## The Number System

# Landmarks in the Hundreds

**Grade 3**

*Also appropriate for Grade 4*

Susan Jo Russell
Andee Rubin

*Developed at TERC, Cambridge, Massachusetts*

**Dale Seymour Publications**

The *Investigations* curriculum was developed at TERC (formerly
Technical Education Research Centers) in collaboration with Kent
State University and the State University of New York at Buffalo.
The work was supported in part by National Science Foundation
Grant No. MDR-9050210. TERC is a nonprofit company working to
improve mathematics and science education. TERC is located at
2067 Massachusetts Avenue, Cambridge, MA 02140.

**This project was supported, in part,**
by the
**National Science Foundation**
Opinions expressed are those of the authors
and not necessarily those of the Foundation

This book is published by Dale Seymour Publications, an imprint of the
Alternative Publishing Group of Addison-Wesley Publishing Company.

Project Editor: Priscilla Cox Samii
Series Editor: Beverly Cory
ESL Consultant: Nancy Sokol Green
Production/Manufacturing Director: Janet Yearian
Production/Manufacturing Coordinator: Barbara Atmore
Design Manager: Jeff Kelly
Design: Don Taka
Illustrations: Jane McCreary, Carl Yoshihara
Composition: Publishing Support Services
Cover: Bay Graphics

 Printed on Recycled Paper

**DALE
SEYMOUR
PUBLICATIONS**
P.O. BOX 10888
PALO ALTO, CA 94303

Order number DS21236
ISBN 0-86651-796-0
  2 3 4 5 6 7 8 9 10-ML-98 97 96 95 94

**T E R C**

*Principal Investigator*  Susan Jo Russell

*Co-Principal Investigator*  Cornelia C. Tierney

*Director of Research and Evaluation*  Jan Mokros

*Curriculum Development*

Joan Akers
Michael T. Battista
Mary Berle-Carman
Douglas H. Clements
Karen Economopoulos
Ricardo Nemirovsky
Andee Rubin
Susan Jo Russell
Cornelia C. Tierney
Amy Shulman Weinberg

*Evaluation and Assessment*

Mary Berle-Carman
Abouali Farmanfarmaian
Jan Mokros
Mark Ogonowski
Amy Shulman Weinberg
Tracey Wright
Lisa Yaffee

*Teacher Development and Support*

Rebecca B. Corwin
Karen Economopoulos
Tracey Wright
Lisa Yaffee

*Technology Development*

Michael T. Battista
Douglas H. Clements
Julie Sarama Meredith
Andee Rubin

*Video Production*

David A. Smith

*Administration and Production*

Amy Catlin
Amy Taber

*Cooperating Classrooms for This Unit*

Corrine Varon
Virginia M. Micciche
Joanne Walcott
Cambridge Public Schools, Cambridge, MA

Angela Philactos
Boston Public Schools, Boston, MA

Jeanne Wall
Linda Harding
Barbara Walsh
Arlington Public Schools, Arlington, MA

Katie Bloomfield
Robert A. Dihlmann
Shutesbury Elementary, Shutesbury, MA

*Consultants and Advisors*

Elizabeth Badger
Deborah Lowenberg Ball
Marilyn Burns
Ann Grady
Joanne M. Gurry
James J. Kaput
Steven Leinwand
Mary M. Lindquist
David S. Moore
John Olive
Leslie P. Steffe
Peter Sullivan
Grayson Wheatley
Virginia Woolley
Anne Zarinnia

*Graduate Assistants*

Kent State University:
Joanne Caniglia, Pam DeLong, Carol King

State University of New York at Buffalo:
Rosa Gonzalez, Sue McMillen,
Julie Sarama Meredith, Sudha Swaminathan

# CONTENTS

## Teacher Notes

*Investigations in Number, Data, and Space* is a K–5 mathematics curriculum with four major goals:

- to offer students meaningful mathematical problems
- to emphasize depth in mathematical thinking rather than superficial exposure to a series of fragmented topics
- to communicate mathematics content and pedagogy to teachers
- to substantially expand the pool of mathematically literate students

The *Investigations* curriculum embodies an approach radically different from the traditional textbook-based curriculum. At each grade level, it consists of a set of separate units, each offering 2–4 weeks of work. These units of study are presented through investigations that involve students in the exploration of major mathematical ideas.

Approaching the mathematics content through investigations helps students develop flexibility and confidence in approaching problems, fluency in using mathematical skills and tools to solve problems, and proficiency in evaluating their solutions. Students also build a repertoire of ways to communicate about their mathematical thinking, while their enjoyment and appreciation of mathematics grows.

The investigations are carefully designed to invite all students into mathematics—girls and boys, diverse cultural, ethnic, and language groups, and students with different strengths and interests. Problem contexts often call on students to share experiences from their family, culture, or community. The curriculum eliminates barriers—such as work in isolation from peers, or emphasis on speed and memorization—that exclude some students from participating successfully in mathematics. The following aspects of the curriculum ensure that all students are included in significant mathematics learning:

- Students spend time exploring problems in depth.
- They find more than one solution to many of the problems they work on.
- They invent their own strategies and approaches, rather than relying on memorized procedures.
- They choose from a variety of concrete materials and appropriate technology, including calculators, as a natural part of their everyday mathematical work.
- They express their mathematical thinking through drawing, writing, and talking.
- They work in a variety of groupings—as a whole class, individually, in pairs, and in small groups.
- They move around the classroom as they explore the mathematics in their environment and talk with their peers.

While reading and other language activities are typically given a great deal of time and emphasis in elementary classrooms, mathematics often does not get the time it needs. If students are to experience mathematics in depth, they must have enough time to become engaged in real mathematical problems. We believe that a minimum of five hours of mathematics classroom time a week—about an hour a day—is critical at the elementary level. The plan and pacing of the *Investigations* curriculum is based on that belief.

For further information about the pedagogy and principles that underlie these investigations, see the Teacher Notes throughout the units and the following books:

- *Implementing the* Investigations in Number, Data, and Space™ *Curriculum*

- *Beyond Arithmetic*

The *Investigations* curriculum is presented through a series of teacher books, one for each unit of study. These books not only provide a complete mathematics curriculum for your students, they offer materials to support your own professional development. You, the teacher, are the person who will make this curriculum come alive in the classroom; the book for each unit is your main support system.

While reproducible resources for students are provided, the curriculum does not include student books. Students work actively with objects and experiences in their own environment and with a variety of manipulative materials and technology, rather than with workbooks and worksheets filled with problems. We also make extensive use of the overhead projector as a way to present problems, to focus group discussion, and to help students share ideas and strategies. If an overhead projector is available, we urge you to try it as suggested in the investigations.

Ultimately, every teacher will use these investigations in ways that make sense for his or her partic-

ular style, the particular group of students, and the constraints and supports of a particular school environment. We have tried to provide with each unit the best information and guidance for a wide variety of situations, drawn from our collaborations with many teachers and students over many years. Our goal in this book is to help you, as a professional educator, implement this mathematics curriculum in a way that will give all your students access to mathematical power.

## Investigation Format

The opening two pages of each investigation help you get ready for the student work that follows. Here you will read:

**What Happens**—a synopsis of each session or block of sessions.

**Mathematical Emphasis**—the most important ideas and processes students will encounter in this investigation.

**What to Plan Ahead of Time**—materials to gather, student sheets to duplicate, transparencies to make, and anything else you need to do before starting.

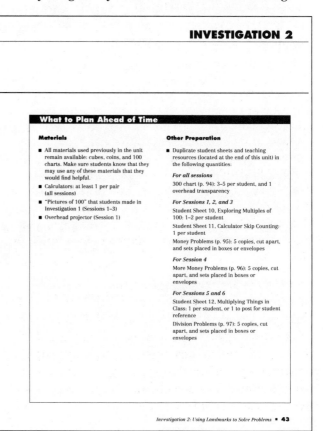

**Sessions** Within an investigation, the activities are organized by class session, a session being a one-hour math class. Sessions are numbered consecutively through an investigation. Often several sessions are grouped together, presenting a block of activities with a single major focus.

When you find a block of sessions presented together—for example, Sessions 1, 2, and 3—read through the entire block first to understand the overall flow and sequence of the activities. Make some preliminary decisions about how you will divide the activities into three sessions for your class, based on what you know about your students. You may need to modify your initial plans as you progress through the activities, and you may want to make notes in the margins of the pages as reminders for the next time you use the unit.

Be sure to read the Session Follow-Up section at the end of the session block to see what homework assignments and extensions are suggested as you make your initial plans.

While you may be used to a curriculum that tells you exactly what each class session should cover, we have found that the teacher is in a better position to make these decisions. Each unit is flexible and may be handled somewhat differently by every teacher. While we provide guidance for how many sessions a particular group of activities is likely to need, we want you to be active in determining an appropriate pace and the best transition points for your class.

**Ten-Minute Math** At the beginning of some sessions, you will find Ten-Minute Math activities. These are designed to be used in tandem with the investigations, but not during the math hour. Rather, we hope you will do them whenever you have a spare 10 minutes—maybe before lunch or recess, or at the end of the day.

Ten-Minute Math offers practice in key concepts, but not always those being covered in the unit. For example, in a unit on using data, Ten-Minute Math might revisit geometric activities done earlier in the year. Complete directions for the suggested activities are included at the end of each unit. A compilation of Ten-Minute Math activities is also available as a separate book.

---

**Sessions 1, 2, and 3**

# Moving Beyond 100

**Materials**

- Students' pictures of 100
- Cubes, coins, and 100 charts
- Money Problems, in sets
- Student Sheet 10 (1–2 per student)
- Student Sheet 11 (1 per student)
- Transparency of 300 chart
- Overhead projector
- 300 chart (2–3 per student)

**What Happens**

After reviewing what they have found out about the factors of 100, students use this knowledge to explore larger numbers. Through a series of activities set up as choices, they explore the multiples of 100 with different tools, including money, the 300 chart, and the calculator. They solve problems involving multiplication and division by 20, 25, and other familiar factors, in the context of money. They examine the patterns in counting by 20's to 1000, and they begin to develop strategies for division using these patterns. Their work focuses on:

- using what they know about 100 to think about multiples of 100
- proving how many groupings of a particular factor make 100

**Ten-Minute Math: Calendar Math** Once or twice during the next few days, do Calendar Math. Remember, Ten-Minute Math activities are designed to be done outside of the math hour.

Ask students to give number combinations that equal the number of the day's date, using multiplication as part of their answer.

List student responses. For example, if the date is January 21, solutions could include $2 \times 10 + 1$, $3 \times 10 - 9$, or $5 \times 5 - 4$.

Choose a "favorite expression" for the day, perhaps the most unusual, or one that uses a new idea. Use this favorite to write the date on the board, for example: January $0 \times 21 + 21$.

For variations, see p. 75.

**Activity**

**Hundreds from Home**

We've been working with the number 100 recently, and we're going to be working with even higher numbers soon. Let's start today by looking at the pictures of 100 you made earlier.

Ask several students to show the arrangements of 100 objects or pictures they made at school and at home. Have them describe how they arranged the items to be able to "prove" that there are exactly 100 objects without counting them one by one.

Spend a bit of time adding by 100's, using the student displays as concrete objects to add. See the **Dialogue Box**, Hundreds from Home (p. 51), for an example. Ask questions such as:

How many 20's are there altogether if we put Jamal's and Annie's together?

**44** ■ *Investigation 2: Using Landmarks to Solve Problems*

---

**Activities** The activities include pair and small-group work, individual tasks, and whole-class discussions. We assume that students are seated together, talking and sharing ideas during all work times. Students most often work cooperatively, although each student may record work individually.

**Choice Time** In some units, some sessions are structured with activity choices. In these cases, students may work simultaneously on different activities focused on the same mathematical ideas. Students choose which activities they want to do, and they cycle through them.

You will need to decide how to set up and introduce these activities and how to let students make their choices. Some teachers present them as station activities, in different parts of the room. Some list the choices on the board as reminders or have students keep their own lists.

**Tips for the Linguistically Diverse Classroom**
At strategic points in each unit, you will find concrete suggestions for simple modifications of the teaching strategies to encourage the participation of all students. Many of these tips offer alternative ways to elicit critical thinking from students at varying levels of English proficiency, as well as from other students who find it difficult to verbalize their thinking.

The tips are supported by suggestions for specific vocabulary work to help ensure that all students can participate fully in the investigations. The Preview for the Linguistically Diverse Classroom (p. 12) lists important words that are assumed as part of the working vocabulary of the unit. Second-language learners will need to become familiar with these words in order to understand the problems and activities they will be doing. These terms can be incorporated into students' second-language work before or during the unit. Activities that can be used to present the words and make them comprehensible are found in the appendix, Vocabulary Support for Second-Language Learners (p. 77).

In addition, ideas for making connections to students' language and cultures, included on the Preview page, help the class explore the unit's concepts from a multicultural perspective.

**Session Follow-Up**

**Homework**  Homework is not given daily for its own sake, but periodically as it makes sense to have follow-up work at home. Homework may be used for (1) review and practice of work done in class; (2) preparation for activities coming up in class—for example, collecting data for a class project; or (3) involving and informing family members.

Some units in the *Investigations* curriculum have more homework than others, simply because it makes sense for the mathematics that's going on. Other units rely on manipulatives that most students won't have at home, making homework difficult. In any case, homework should always be directly connected to the investigations in the unit, or to work in previous units—never sheets of problems just to keep students busy.

**Extensions**  These follow-up activities are opportunities for some or all students to explore a topic in greater depth or in a different context. They are not designed for "fast" students; mathematics is a multifaceted discipline, and different students will want to go further in different investigations. Look for and encourage the sparks of interest and enthusiasm you see in your students, and use the extensions to help them pursue these interests.

**Family Letter**  A letter that you can send home to students' families is included with the blackline masters for each unit. We want families to be informed about the mathematics work in your classroom; they should be encouraged to participate in and support their children's work. A reminder to send home the letter appears in one of the early investigations. (These letters are also available separately in the following languages: Spanish, Vietnamese, Cantonese, Hmong, and Cambodian.)

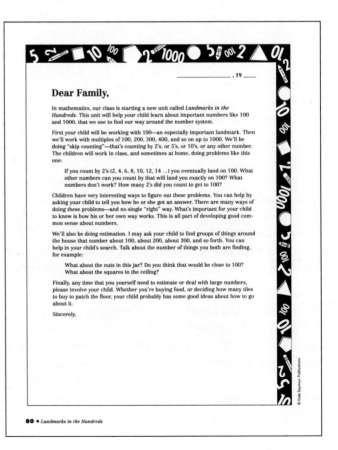

## Materials

A complete list of the materials needed for the unit is found on p. 10. Some of these materials are available in a kit for the *Investigations* grade 3 curriculum. Individual items can also be purchased as needed from school supply stores and dealers.

In an active mathematics classroom, certain basic materials should be available at all times: interlocking cubes, pencils, unlined paper, graph paper, calculators, things to count with, and measuring tools. Some activities in this curriculum require scissors and glue sticks or tape. Stick-on notes and large paper are also useful materials throughout.

So that students can independently get what they need at any time, they should know where these materials are kept, how they are stored, and how they are to be returned to the storage area. For example, interlocking cubes are best stored in towers of ten; then, whatever the activity, they should be returned to storage in groups of ten at the end of the hour. You'll find that establishing such routines at the beginning of the year is well worth the time and effort.

## Student Sheets and Teaching Resources

Reproducible pages to help you teach the unit are found at the end of this book. These include masters for making overhead transparencies and other teaching tools, as well as student recording sheets.

Many of the field-test teachers requested more sheets to help students record their work, and we have tried to be responsive to this need. At the same time, we think it's important that students find their own ways of organizing and recording their work. They need to learn how to explain their thinking with both drawings and written words, and how to organize their results so someone else can understand them.

To ensure that students get a chance to learn how to represent and organize their own work, we deliberately do not provide student sheets for every activity. We recommend that your students keep a mathematics notebook or folder so that their work, whether on reproducible sheets or their own paper, is always available to them for reference.

Name                                          Date

### Ways to Split Up a Dollar

| Number of People Sharing a Dollar | How Much Each Person Gets |
|---|---|
|  |  |
|  |  |
|  |  |
|  |  |
|  |  |
|  |  |
|  |  |
|  |  |
|  |  |
|  |  |
|  |  |

Cannot split a dollar evenly:

© Dale Seymour Publications

*Landmarks in the Hundreds* ▪ **89**

## Help for You, the Teacher

Because we believe strongly that a new curriculum must help teachers think in new ways about mathematics and about their students' mathematical thinking processes, we have included a great deal of material to help you learn more about both.

**About the Mathematics in This Unit** This introductory section (p. 11) summarizes for you the critical information about the mathematics you will be teaching. This will be particularly valuable to teachers who are accustomed to a traditional textbook-based curriculum.

**Teacher Notes** These reference notes provide practical information about the mathematics you are teaching and about our experience with how students learn. Many of the notes were written in response to actual questions from teachers, or to discuss important things we saw happening in the field-test classrooms. Some teachers like to read them all before starting the unit, then review them as they come up in particular investigations.

**Dialogue Boxes** Sample dialogues throughout the unit demonstrate how students typically express their mathematical ideas, what issues and confusions arise in their thinking, and how some teachers have guided class discussions.

These dialogues are based on the extensive classroom testing of this curriculum; many are word-for-word transcriptions of recorded class discussions. They are not always easy reading; sometimes it may take some effort to unravel what the students are trying to say. But this is the value of these dialogues; they offer good clues to how your students may develop and express their approaches and strategies, helping you prepare for your own class discussions.

**Where to Start** You may not have time to read everything the first time you use this unit. As a first-time user, you will likely focus on understanding the activities and working them out with your students. Read completely through each investigation before starting to present it.

When you next teach this same unit, you can begin to read more of the background. Each time you present this unit, you will learn more about how your students understand the mathematical ideas. The first-time user of *Landmarks in the Hundreds* should read the following:

- About the Mathematics in This Unit (p. 11)
- Teacher Note: Students' Problems with Skip Counting (p. 26)
- Teacher Note: Introducing Mathematical Vocabulary (p. 27)
- Teacher Note: What About Notation? (p. 33)
- Dialogue Box: How Many 20's in 280? (p. 52)

**Teacher Checkpoints** As a teacher of the *Investigations* curriculum, you observe students daily, listen to their discussions, look carefully at their work, and use this information to guide your teaching. We have designated Teacher Checkpoints as natural times to get an overall sense of how your class is doing in the unit.

The Teacher Checkpoints provide a time for you to pause and reflect on your teaching plan while observing students at work in an activity. These sections offer tips on what you should be looking for and how you might adjust your pacing. Are most students fluent with strategies for solving a particular kind of problem? Are they just starting to formulate good strategies? Or are they still struggling with how to start?

Depending on what you see as the students work, you may want to spend more time on similar problems, change some of the problems to use smaller numbers, move quickly to more challenging material, modify subsequent activities for some students, work on particular ideas with a small group, or pair students who have good strategies with those who are having more difficulty.

In *Landmarks in the Hundreds* you will find two Teacher Checkpoints:

Showing Factors of 36 or 48 (p. 24)
Factors of 100 (p. 39)

**Embedded Assessment Activities** Use the built-in assessments included in this unit to help you examine the work of individual students, figure out what it means, and provide feedback. From the students' point of view, the activities you will be using for assessment are no different from any others; they don't look or feel like traditional tests.

These activities sometimes involve writing and reflecting, at other times a brief interaction between student and teacher, and in still other instances the creation and explanation of a product.

In *Landmarks in the Hundreds* you will find assessment activities in the second and third investigations:

How Many in 500? (p. 48)
Calculating with the 1000 Chart (p. 70)

Teachers find the hardest part of the assessment to be interpreting their students' work. If you have used a process approach to teaching writing, you will find our mathematics approach familiar. To help with interpretation, we provide guidelines and questions to ask about the students' work. In some cases we include a Teacher Note with specific examples of student work and a commentary on what it indicates. This framework can help you determine how your students are progressing.

As you evaluate students' work, it's important to remember that you're looking for much more than the "right answer." You'll want to know what their strategies are for solving the problem, how well these strategies work, whether they can keep track of and logically organize an approach to the problem, and how they make use of representations and tools to solve the problem.

**Ongoing Assessment** Good assessment of student work involves a combination of approaches. Some of the things you might do on an ongoing basis include the following:

- **Observation** Circulate around the room to observe students as they work. Watch for the development of their mathematical strategies, and listen to their discussions of mathematical ideas.

- **Portfolios** Ask students to document their work, in journals, notebooks, or portfolios. Periodically review this work to see how their mathematical thinking and writing are changing. Some teachers have students keep a notebook or folder for each unit, while others prefer one mathematics notebook or a portfolio of selected work for the entire year. Take time at the end of each unit for students to choose work for their portfolios. You might also have them write about what they've learned in the unit.

# Landmarks in the Hundreds

**Content of This Unit**   Students work with 100, factors of 100, and multiples of 100 (up to 1000). They use coins, 100 charts, and cubes to investigate these numbers. They develop a sense of these quantities by counting real objects and by making "pictures" of 100 and 1000. They develop their own strategies, based on what they know about these landmark numbers, to solve multiplication and division problems.

**Connections with Other Units**   If you are doing the full-year *Investigations* curriculum in the suggested sequence for grade 3, this is the fifth of ten units. Your class will have already completed the Multiplication and Division unit *Things That Come in Groups.* There, students practiced skip counting by 2's, 3's, 4's, 5's, and 6's, and worked on such problems as "how many 4's in 48?" If your students have not had comparable experience, spend more time on the first three sessions of Investigation 1. During Investigation 2, these students may also need to spend more time working with multiples of 10 and with the smaller multiples of 100.

If your school is not using the full-year curriculum, this unit can also be used successfully at grade 4. The work in this unit is continued and extended in the grade 4–5 unit, *Landmarks in the Thousands.*

## *Investigations* Curriculum ■ Suggested Grade 3 Sequence

*Mathematical Thinking at Grade 3* (Introduction)

*Things That Come in Groups* (Multiplication and Division)

*Flips, Turns, and Area* (2-D Geometry)

*From Paces to Feet* (Measuring and Data)

▶ *Landmarks in the Hundreds* (The Number System)

*Up and Down the Number Line* (Changes)

*Combining and Comparing* (Addition and Subtraction)

*Turtle Paths* (2-D Geometry)

*Fair Shares* (Fractions)

*Exploring Solids and Boxes* (3-D Geometry)

## Investigation 1 • Finding Factors

| Class Sessions | Activities | Pacing | Ten-Minute Math |
|---|---|---|---|
| Session 1<br>SKIP COUNTING WITH CUBES | Ways to Count to 10<br>Finding Factors with Cubes<br>■ Homework | 1 hr | |
| Sessions 2 and 3<br>FACTORS OF 24, 36, AND 48 | Skip Counting on the 100 Chart<br>What's a Factor?<br>Making Counting Charts for 24<br>Factors of 36 and 48<br>■ Teacher Checkpoint: Showing Factors of<br>   36 or 48<br>What Did You Find Out About 24, 36, and 48?<br>■ Homework | 2 hrs | Counting<br>Around<br>the Class |
| Sessions 4 and 5<br>FACTORS OF 100 | What Numbers Are Factors of 100?<br>Making a Picture of 100<br>■ Homework | 2 hrs | |
| Sessions 6 and 7<br>DIVIDING A DOLLAR | Listing the Factors of 100<br>Working with Coins<br>Dividing a Dollar Among Five People<br>How Can We Divide a Dollar Evenly?<br>■ Teacher Checkpoint: Factors of 100 | 2 hrs | |

## Investigation 2 • Using Landmarks to Solve Problems

| Class Sessions | Activities | Pacing | Ten-Minute Math |
|---|---|---|---|
| Sessions 1, 2, and 3<br>MOVING BEYOND 100 | Hundreds from Home<br>Choice Time: Exploring Multiples of 100<br>Finding Patterns in the 20's<br>■ Assessment: How Many in 500?<br>■ Homework | 3 hrs | |
| Session 4<br>SOLVING PROBLEMS WITH MONEY | Class Discussion: Six People Paying $1.50 Each<br>Problems Using Money<br>■ Homework | 1 hr | Calendar<br>Math |
| Sessions 5 and 6<br>REAL-WORLD MULTIPLYING<br>AND DIVIDING | Using Standard Notation for Division<br>Choice Time: Working with Landmarks<br>Multiplying and Dividing on the Calculator<br>■ Homework<br>■ Extensions | 2 hrs | |

*Continued on next page*

| Investigation 3 • Constructing a 1000 Chart | | | |
|---|---|---|---|
| **Class Sessions** | **Activities** | **Pacing** | **Ten-Minute Math** |
| Session 1<br>A 1000 CHART | Making a Thousand<br>■ Homework | 1 hr | ◑<br>Counting Around the Class |
| Sessions 2 and 3<br>FINDING LARGE QUANTITIES | Locating Numbers on the 1000 Chart<br>Finding Real Quantities for the 1000 Chart<br>■ Assessment: Calculating with the 1000 Chart | 2 hrs | |

## MATERIALS LIST

Following are the basic materials needed for the activities in this unit. The suggested quantities are ideal; however, in some instances you can work with smaller quantities by running several activities, requiring different materials, simultaneously.

Items marked with an asterisk are provided with the *Investigations* Materials Kit for grade 3.

* Interlocking cubes: at least 50 per student pair

* Plastic coins: at least 50 pennies, 25 nickels, 12 dimes, and 6 quarters per small group of students (real coins may be substituted or used in addition to these)

Calculators: at least 1 per pair of students

* Small counters or cubes (1 cm): 1 per student

*Two Ways to Count to Ten*, retold by Ruby Dee (Holt, 1988) (optional)

Large poster or chart paper: 1 sheet per pair of students

Colored paper, scrap materials

Scissors, glue or paste, tape, crayons or markers

String or ribbon (optional)

Overhead projector

The following materials are provided at the end of this unit as blackline masters. They are also available in classroom sets.

Family Letter (p. 80)

Student Sheets 1–12 (pp. 81–92)

Teaching Resources:

    100 Chart (p. 93)

    300 Chart (p. 94)

    Money Problems (p. 95)

    More Money Problems (p. 96)

    Division Problems (p. 97)

    One-Centimeter Graph Paper (p. 98)

An important part of students' mathematical work in the elementary grades is building an understanding of the base ten number system. This unit provides activities that develop knowledge about important *landmarks* in that system—numbers that are familiar landing places, that make for simple calculations, and to which other numbers can be related.

Because our number system is based on powers of ten, the numbers 10, 100, 1000, and their multiples are especially important landmarks. In solving real problems, people with well-developed number sense draw on their knowledge of these important landmarks. For example, think about how you would solve this problem, in your head, before you continue reading:

> If there are about 25 students in a class and 17 classes in our school, about how many students are there altogether?

Many people would use their knowledge that there are four 25's in every 100 to help them solve this problem mentally. Rather than multiplying 17 by 25, they will think something like this: "Four 25's in 100, eight in 200, 12, 16, that's 400, and one more 25 makes 425."

Knowledge about 10, 100, 1000, their multiples, and their factors is the basis of good number sense. As students learn about 100, how to take it apart into its factors, and how to use it to construct other numbers, they gain the knowledge they need to develop their own strategies to solve problems using quantities in the hundreds. They develop good estimation strategies and are less likely to make the kinds of errors that result from the use of faulty algorithms.

For example, a student who has developed knowledge about 20 and its relationship to 100, who has experience counting by 20's, and knows what the pattern of the multiples of 20 is like, would never make this common error:

$$
\begin{array}{r}
440 \\
-\ 380 \\
\hline
140
\end{array}
$$

Using a written subtraction algorithm—whether faulty or correct—is not a sensible approach to solving this problem. Rather, by inspecting the numbers and using knowledge of important landmarks in the number system, students should eventually be able to solve this problem mentally with no trouble:

> "380 to 400 is 20, then 20, 40, two more 20's gets to 440, so that's three 20's. The answer is 60."

**Mathematical Emphasis**  At the beginning of each investigation, the Mathematical Emphasis section tells you what is most important for students to learn about during that investigation. Many of these mathematical understandings and processes are difficult and complex. Students gradually learn more and more about each idea over many years of schooling. Individual students will begin and end the unit with different levels of knowledge and skill, but all will gain greater knowledge about 100 and multiples of 100 and develop strategies for solving problems involving these important numbers.

In the *Investigations* curriculum, mathematical vocabulary is introduced naturally during the activities. We don't ask students to learn definitions of new terms; rather, they come to understand such words as *factor* or *area* or *symmetry* by hearing them used frequently in discussion as they investigate new concepts. This approach is compatible with current theories of second-language acquisition, which emphasize the use of new vocabulary in meaningful contexts while students are actively involved with objects, pictures, and physical movement.

Listed below are some key words used in this unit that will not be new to most English speakers at this age level, but may be unfamiliar to students with limited English proficiency. You will want to spend additional time working on these words with your students who are learning English. If your students are working with a second-language teacher, you might enlist your colleague's aid in familiarizing students with these words, before and during this unit. In the classroom, look for opportunities for students to hear and use these words. Activities you can use to present the words are given in the appendix, Vocabulary Support for Second-Language Learners (p. 77).

**the numbers 1 to 100** Students use the 100 chart throughout the unit. They should be able to write the numerals and identify each by name.

**divide, group, equal, unequal** As students learn about factors in this unit, they *divide* collections of cubes or amounts of money into *equal groups.*

**money: coins, cents, nickel, dime, quarter, dollar** In order to "divide a dollar evenly among five people," students need to recognize U.S. coins and know the value of each.

**pattern** Finding patterns is a key mathematical process. In this unit, students look for visual patterns on the 100 chart (for example, the diagonal pattern created when skip counting by 3's) and for number patterns (for example, when counting by 5's, alternating numbers end in 5 and 0).

## Multicultural Extensions for All Students

Whenever possible, encourage students to share words, objects, customs, or any aspects of daily life from their own cultures and backgrounds that are relevant to the activities in this unit. For example:

- Students who have coins from their countries of origin can bring them to show to the class. They might make a poster showing equivalencies of the coins in these monetary systems.

- When students are making up their own word problems, encourage them to write problems that are based on aspects of their cultures— foods, games and sports that involve teams, and so forth.

# Investigations

# Finding Factors

## What Happens

**Session 1: Skip Counting with Cubes** Students are introduced to skip counting using interlocking cubes. By arranging 20 cubes in equal groups, they find and record "ways to make 20" (they are finding *factors*, but that term is not introduced until Session 2). Students also record groupings they try that "won't work to make 20." They use their cubes to find groupings (factors) for at least one other number.

**Sessions 2 and 3: Factors of 24, 36, and 48** These sessions begin with some work to introduce or review skip counting using a 100 chart. Then students are introduced to the term *factor* through discussion of their work with 20 in the previous session. Students find factors of 24, 36, and 48 and discuss what they notice about the factors of these numbers. Students record their findings by skip counting on a partial 100 chart and by using multiplication notation.

**Sessions 4 and 5: Factors of 100** Students find factors of 100. They make a set of 100 charts for the numbers that are factors of one hundred, skip counting by one factor on each chart. They make a display showing 100 things, grouped by one of the factors of 100. They make a second display, grouped by a different factor, at home.

**Sessions 6 and 7: Dividing a Dollar** The class lists and discusses all the factors of 100 they have found. Students use coins to explore how to share a dollar equally among five people, then investigate ways to divide a dollar evenly among different numbers of people.

## Mathematical Emphasis

- Understanding the relationship between skip counting and grouping (for example, as we count 3, 6, 9, 12, we are adding a group of 3 to the total each time)

- Becoming familiar with the relationships among commonly encountered factors and multiples (for example, is 3 a factor of 24? how many 3's does it take to make 24?)

- Increasing fluency in counting by single-digit numbers (2's, 3's, 4's, 6's, 8's) as well as by useful two-digit numbers (10's, 20's, 25's)

- Developing familiarity with the factors of 100, an important landmark in our number system, and their relationships to 100 (for example, that there are twenty 5's in 100 and five 20's in 100) through work with cubes, coins, and 100 charts

## What to Plan Ahead of Time

### Materials

- *Two Ways to Count to Ten*, retold by Ruby Dee (Holt, 1988) (Session 1, optional)
- Interlocking cubes: at least 50 per pair (Sessions 1–5)
- Overhead projector (Sessions 2–4)
- Art materials for making pictures of 100: colored paper, scissors, glue or paste, crayons or markers, any scrap materials available (Sessions 4–5)
- Plastic or real coins: at least 50 pennies, 25 nickels, 12 dimes, and 6 quarters per small group of students. If using plastic, try to include at least one collection of real coins and let the groups take turns using them. Also, prepare another small sample of coins for each student pair: a few pennies, nickels, dimes, and one quarter, in differing total amounts from about 48 to 60 cents, in a plastic bag, envelope, or paper cup. (Sessions 6–7)

### Other Preparation

- Duplicate student sheets and teaching resources (located at the end of this unit) in the following quantities:

  *For Session 1*
  Student Sheet 1, Ways to Make 20: 2 per student

  Student Sheet 2, Ways to Make __: 4 per student (2 for homework)

  Family letter (p.80): 1 per student. Remember to sign it before copying.

  *For Sessions 2 and 3*
  100 chart (p. 93): 2 per student (optional), and 1 overhead transparency

  Student Sheet 3, Factors of 24: 2 per pair, and 1 overhead transparency

  Student Sheet 4, Factors of 36: 3 per pair

  Student Sheet 5, Factors of 48: 3 per pair

  *For Sessions 4 and 5*
  Student Sheet 6, Miniature 100 Charts: 2 per student

  Student Sheet 7, Factors of 100: 1 per student

  Student Sheet 8, A Picture of 100: 1 per student (homework)

  *For Sessions 6 and 7*
  Student Sheet 9, Ways to Split Up a Dollar: 1 per student

- If you plan to provide folders in which students will save their work for the entire unit, prepare these for distribution during Session 1.

# Skip Counting with Cubes

## Materials

- *Two Ways to Count to Ten* (optional)
- Interlocking cubes (40 per pair)
- Student Sheet 1 (2 per student)
- Student Sheet 2 (4 per student)
- Family letter (1 per student)

## What Happens

Students are introduced to skip counting using interlocking cubes. By arranging 20 cubes in equal groups, they find and record "ways to make 20" (they are finding *factors*, but that term is not introduced until Session 2). Students also record groupings they try that "won't work to make 20." They use their cubes to find groupings (factors) for at least one other number. Their work focuses on:

- finding factors by making equal groups
- recording their work using pictures and numbers

## Activity

### Ways to Count to 10

If you have *Two Ways to Count to Ten* (a Liberian folktale), read the story as an introduction to skip counting. In this tale, the leopard holds a contest to choose his successor as king of the jungle. Each animal must throw a spear high up into the air. The animal who can count to ten before the spear reaches the ground will be the winner; he will be named prince and will marry the leopard's daughter. None of the animals succeeds until the clever antelope counts by 2's.

**Did the animals think of all the ways to count to 10? Are there any others?**

If you don't have the book, you might want to tell this story in your own words, or simply ask the class how many ways they can think of to count to ten:

**I know you can all count to ten—1, 2, 3, 4, 5, 6, 7, 8, 9, 10—but I'm thinking of a special way to count to 10. It's like a shortcut that gets us there faster. Who can think of a special way to count to 10?**

If students don't have any ideas, you might suggest:

**Is there a way I could do it starting with 2 instead of with 1?**

Count together by 2's. Can students think of any other ways to count to 10?

# Finding Factors with Cubes

**Building 20 with Groups of Cubes**   Give each student or pair of students 20 interlocking cubes and two copies of Student Sheet 1, Ways to Make 20. Students find as many ways as they can to build 20 using equal groups of cubes. For example, they might build 20 out of 2's:

They record on Student Sheet 1 all the groupings they find that work and that don't work. For the groupings that do work, students both draw their cubes and record counting by that number, for example:

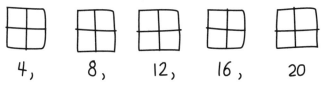

4,      8,      12,      16,      20

As you watch students work, make sure that they record all the groupings they try, even the ones that don't work. If a student announces "I'm finished," ask questions to prompt further thinking:

**Do you think you have all the ways? Why do you think so? Do you think 8 might work? How do you know?**

---

Name  Elena                        Date  Jan. 5

**Student Sheet 1**

### Ways to Make 20

Take 20 cubes. Put them in equal groups.
How many different ways can you make 20?
Record your results here.

| Numbers I tried that will make 20 |
|---|

Number of cubes in group: 2
Picture of 20:

Count:  2, 4, 6, 8, 10, 12, 14, 16, 18, 20

Number of cubes in group: ___
Picture of 20:

Count:  5, 10, 15, 20

Number of cubes in group: ___

**Building More Numbers**   Distribute two copies of Student Sheet 2, Ways to Make ___, to each student. Have students choose another number to work with and write it in the blank in the title. Using the cubes, they find all the groupings that work to make their new number, just as they did for 20. Students can work in pairs or individually.

Help individual students choose a number appropriate for them. If 20 offered about the right level of challenge, those students could go on to 28 or 32. If 20 was difficult for them, they might try 12 or 16. Students who need a greater challenge might try larger numbers (40, 50, 60) or numbers with less familiar factors (21, 35, 42). **Note:** Don't use 24, 36, or 48, because students will work with these in later sessions.

As you circulate, ask students to show and tell you how they know a particular number "works." Encourage them to keep looking if they have not found all the possible groupings that work. Some students may not realize that they can count by numbers greater than 10, so remind them that they can.

## Session 1 Follow-Up

 **Homework**

Send home the family letter with two clean copies of Student Sheet 2. For homework, students find groupings that work for yet another number. Help students choose a number at an appropriate level of difficulty. Briefly discuss with students objects they might use to count with at home: pennies, blocks, buttons, paper clips, pebbles, or drawings of dots on paper.

# Factors of 24, 36, and 48

## What Happens

These sessions begin with some work to introduce or review skip counting using a 100 chart. Then students are introduced to the term *factor* through discussion of their work with 20 in the previous session. Students find factors of 24, 36, and 48 and discuss what they notice about the factors of these numbers. Students record their findings by skip counting on a partial 100 chart and by using multiplication notation. Their work focuses on:

- finding factors by skip counting

- exploring the relationship between a multiple and its factors (how many 3's does it take to make 24?)

- developing facility in counting by 2's, 3's, 4's, 6's, and 8's

- making conjectures about factors and multiples (you can always use the number itself; 0 is never a factor; 2 is always a factor of any even number)

- using multiplication notation to record work with factors

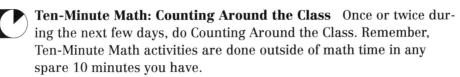 **Ten-Minute Math: Counting Around the Class**  Once or twice during the next few days, do Counting Around the Class. Remember, Ten-Minute Math activities are done outside of math time in any spare 10 minutes you have.

Choose a number to count by, let's say 3. Ask students to predict what number they'll land on if they count around the class exactly once. Encourage students to talk about how they could figure this out without doing the actual counting.

Then start the count: The first student says "3," the next "6," the next "9," and so forth. If students seem unfamiliar with what comes next, you may want to put numbers on the board as they count, so they can begin to see patterns.

Stop two or three times during the count to ask a question like this:

**We're at 33—how many students have counted so far?**

After counting around once, compare the actual ending number with their predictions.

For variations on this activity, see p. 73.

## Materials

- 100 chart (2 per student, optional)
- Transparency of 100 chart (optional)
- Interlocking cubes (50+ per pair)
- Transparency of Student Sheet 3
- Student Sheet 3 (2 per pair)
- Student Sheet 4 (3 per pair)
- Student Sheet 5 (3 per pair)
- Overhead projector

# Skip Counting on the 100 Chart

Consider the following to decide how much emphasis to give this activity:

■ If your students have *not* done skip counting on a 100 chart, they need to do this activity.

■ If your students did skip counting earlier in the year but could use some review and practice, you might try the activity with some less familiar numbers—6, 7, 8, or 9.

■ If your students have recently done a lot of skip counting on the 100 chart, you can go on to the next activity, What's a Factor? (p. 22).

**Counting by 2's**   Introduce or reacquaint your students with skip counting on the 100 chart. Showing the overhead transparency of the 100 chart, ask students to help you count by 2's. As the students tell you the next number in the series (2, 4, 6, 8, 10, 12, 14 …), circle or put an X on it. When you get up to about 24, ask:

**As you're counting, how do you know what comes next?**

Encourage a variety of responses. Even though one student has already given a correct answer, ask other students for their way of thinking about it. Some students will begin to notice patterns on the 100 chart:

It's only the even numbers.

You just keep going under the ones you've already done.

You skip every other number.

Probably both you and your students will naturally use several different ways to refer to what you're doing on the 100 chart, such as "skip count by 2's," "count by 2's," "do the 2's pattern." This variety of language is valuable, as long as students understand that the phrases all refer to the same activity.

Distribute student copies of the 100 chart and have students complete the 2's pattern there. Circulate quickly and help students with any difficulties they may be having. Encourage them to double-check by comparing charts with each other. See the **Teacher Note**, Students' Problems with Skip Counting (p. 26); in particular, read about encouraging students to use cubes to build the groupings as they count.

Ask students to share the patterns they see.

**Counting by 3's**   Using a second copy of the 100 chart, students now count by 3's on their own. To help them get started, you might have them tell you the first few numbers of the 3's pattern, up to about 15, while you mark them on a clean transparency.

While students are working on their 3's, fill in the transparency by 3's up to 30. When students are finished with their own charts, ask:

**What are some ways you can tell what number comes next on my chart?**

| 1 | 2 | 3 | 4 | 5 | 6 | 7 | 8 | 9 | 10 |
|---|---|---|---|---|---|---|---|---|---|
| 11 | 12 | 13 | 14 | 15 | 16 | 17 | 18 | 19 | 20 |
| 21 | 22 | 23 | 24 | 25 | 26 | 27 | 28 | 29 | 30 |
| 31 | 32 | 33 | 34 | 35 | 36 | 37 | 38 | 39 | 40 |
| 41 | 42 | 43 | 44 | 45 | 46 | 47 | 48 | 49 | 50 |
| 51 | 52 | 53 | 54 | 55 | 56 | 57 | 58 | 59 | 60 |
| 61 | 62 | 63 | 64 | 65 | 66 | 67 | 68 | 69 | 70 |
| 71 | 72 | 73 | 74 | 75 | 76 | 77 | 78 | 79 | 80 |
| 81 | 82 | 83 | 84 | 85 | 86 | 87 | 88 | 89 | 90 |
| 91 | 92 | 93 | 94 | 95 | 96 | 97 | 98 | 99 | 100 |

Responses might include:

> Count three more from 30.
> It's the next one in the diagonal, 6, 15, 24, 33.
> It's just like the first line—it's going to go 3, 6, 9 again.

Keep asking until there are no more suggestions.

Now fill in your own chart up to 63. Ask the students what ways they can think of to predict the next number.

When the counting is completed, ask students what patterns they can see in counting by 3's. Let them point out patterns on the transparency. Discuss further:

**How is the 3's pattern different from the 2's pattern?**

## What's a Factor?

Make a class list of all the numbers that make equal groupings for 20 (those that the class discovered in Session 1). These are the *factors* of 20. They include 1, 2, 4, 5, 10, and 20. Also list numbers students tried that did not work for 20. Pose questions for discussion:

**How do you know that 3 doesn't work? How did you find out that 20 works? Were there any numbers that surprised you? Do you think we have all the factors of 20? Could there be any others? Why do you think so?**

In this discussion, begin to use the word *factor*, but don't insist that students use this word. See the **Teacher Note**, Introducing Mathematical Vocabulary (p. 27).

❖ **Tip for the Linguistically Diverse Classroom** Instead of asking students to articulate their answers, ask them to communicate their thoughts by using visual aids, either cubes or marks on the board. For example:

**Show that 3 is NOT** [*shake head*] **a factor of 20.**

Student groups 20 cubes or marks on the board as follows:

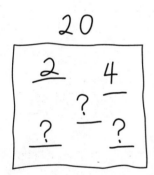

As students agree on numbers that are factors of 20, write them inside a square with the number 20 written above it. Add question marks with lines beneath them inside the square. Pointing to these lines, ask if there might be more factors for [*point*] 20. If students think so, have them come forward, erase the question marks, and write these numbers on the blank lines. Challenge them to prove that these numbers are indeed factors.

## Making Counting Charts for 24

Each pair of students needs a supply of cubes and two copies of Student Sheet 3, Factors of 24.

**We're going to try to find all the factors of 24. What's a number that we can count by to land exactly on 24?**

Take a student suggestion. Ask students to count by that number to 24. Using the overhead transparency of Student Sheet 3, mark the numbers as they count. Then focus on how many of that number it would take to make 24. For example, if they counted by 2's, ask:

**If you built 24 out of 2's, how many 2's would you need?**

Ask students to prove their answer by using the cubes. As students work, circulate quickly to see if most can show that twelve 2's make 24.

Finally, ask students how they could write this result using a multiplication sentence. If they don't know, show them this sentence:

$12 \times 2 = 24$

Explain that it can be read as "12 groups of 2 makes 24."

See the **Teacher Note**, What About Notation? (p. 33), for more information on helping students understand the connection between the relationships they are showing with cubes or counting charts and standard multiplication and division notation.

Next introduce the student sheet activity:

**Mathematicians think of 24 as a special number because it has a lot of factors. You're going to see how many factors of 24 you can find. For each factor, use one of the counting charts on Student Sheet 3. Show how you count by that number on the chart, then fill in the sentences that tell about that factor.**

Students work in pairs to find the factors of 24. Since there are eight factors of 24 (1, 2, 3, 4, 6, 8, 12, 24), each pair will need two copies of Student Sheet 3.

I found a secret! If you count by 24, you land right on 24!

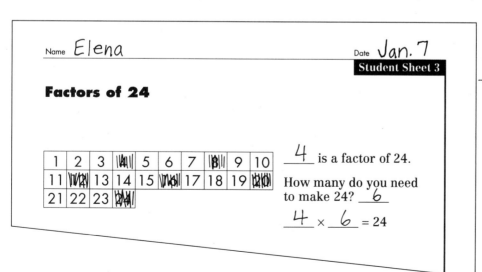

Name _Elena_                    Date _Jan. 7_

Student Sheet 3

**Factors of 24**

| 1 | 2 | 3 | 4 | 5 | 6 | 7 | 8 | 9 | 10 |
|---|---|---|---|---|---|---|---|---|----|
| 11 | 12 | 13 | 14 | 15 | 16 | 17 | 18 | 19 | 20 |
| 21 | 22 | 23 | 24 | | | | | | |

_4_ is a factor of 24.

How many do you need to make 24? _6_

_4_ × _6_ = 24

# Factors of 36 and 48

**Making Charts for 36 or 48**   Distribute three copies of Student Sheet 4, Factors of 36, and Student Sheet 5, Factors of 48, to each student pair. Students continue as in the preceding activity, marking charts for the factors of either 36 or 48. Many students will work on just one of these numbers; some students might want to work on both. You might assign one of the numbers for homework, in which case students will need their own copies of the student sheet.

Encourage discussion within small groups of students working near each other. What are they finding out about 24, 36, and 48? Are there similarities, differences? Note any interesting observations and encourage students to contribute these later to the whole-class discussion.

## Teacher Checkpoint

## Showing Factors of 36 or 48

At some point while students are working on their 36 and 48 charts, stop the whole class and ask everyone to do the following:

**Use your cubes to show me one of the ways to count to either 36 or to 48. You should arrange your cubes in such a way that I can tell, just by looking at your cubes, what factor you chose and whether it makes 36 or 48.**

Give students a few minutes to arrange their cubes. Once the cubes are arranged, students can leave them in place and go back to their work on the 36 and 48 charts while you circulate. As you walk around to take a quick look at each student's work, your role is to be the audience:

**Let's see if I can tell how you counted by looking at what each of you did with the cubes.**

You can also ask individual students how many groups they needed to make the total:

**I see you used 4's to make 36. Do you know how many 4's you needed?**

This brief check will give you a chance to reflect on how comfortable the class as a whole is becoming with finding factors and relating them to the multiple with which they are working. Do students understand that when they skip count by a number, they are accumulating groups of that number of objects? Can they skip count easily using the grouping they have chosen?

## Class Discussion: What Did You Find Out About 24, 36, and 48?

When students have worked on at least two of these numbers, have a brief class discussion in which students describe what they have noticed about the factors of these numbers. You don't need to wait until students are finished with all the student sheets in order to have this discussion.

This is a good time to share observations that you have heard made by individual students or in small groups.

❖ **Tip for the Linguistically Diverse Classroom** Include discussion questions that can be simply answered by a hand-showing or yes/no response. For example:

> Raise your hand if you think 24 and 36 share some of the same factors.
>
> Is 2 a factor of both 24 and 36?

Fill squares with the factors of 24 and 36. Ask students to point to the factors in the squares that are the same.

At this point, students will probably come up with some general conjectures about factors. You may want to make a class list of these to keep (see the **Dialogue Box**, Factors of 24, 36, and 48, page 25). List any ideas that students feel they have good evidence for now, even though the ideas may need to be tested further. You can return periodically to these conjectures throughout the unit.

## Sessions 2 and 3 Follow-Up

Students can take home Student Sheet 4, Factors of 36, or Student Sheet 5, Factors of 48, to complete as homework if they do not finish in class. Remember that students will need three copies of each sheet.

🏠 **Homework**

Some students have difficulty keeping track of their skip counting on the 100 chart. Here are some confusions we have noticed in classrooms:

- Some students always start on 1, no matter which number they are skip counting by.

- The count may get off by 1 because the student pauses at a circled number, then starts counting again with that number. For example, when counting by 6's, a student counts 6, 12, 18, then begins the next count on 18. After counting six more numbers (18, 19, 20, 21, 22, 23), the student lands on 23 instead of 24.

- Students sometimes follow a "false pattern" that doesn't actually work for the number they are counting by. For example, they may circle 3, 6, 9, then color straight down the columns under the 3, 6, and 9, not realizing that the 3's pattern doesn't continue in columns the way the 2's pattern does.

- Students may miscount one interval and then continue counting correctly, so that all subsequent numbers are affected by the original mistake. For example: 3, 6, 9, 12, 15, 19, 22, 25, 28 ....

Some of these difficulties are simply miscounting mistakes that anyone can make. Help students to use the pattern on their counting charts to check: Does the pattern continue consistently on the chart? Also, have students double-check each other. When two or three students compare charts, they can often find and correct their own miscounting.

However, some students may truly not understand what they are doing when they "count by 2's" or "count by 3's" on their charts. Here, using cubes as a first step will help. That is, when counting by 2's, the student makes a group of 2 cubes, then marks 2 on the chart; makes another group of 2 cubes (perhaps in a different color), and marks the total, 4; then makes another group of cubes, marks the total, 6; and so forth. Students will naturally stop using the cubes as soon as they feel comfortable with skip counting.

We have found that it's not helpful for students to use cubes to mark squares directly on the counting charts. Students can't see the numbers underneath them, and they often move a cube accidentally to a neighboring square, thereby misleading themselves about the pattern on the chart.

# Introducing Mathematical Vocabulary

In this unit, several important mathematical words come up naturally in discussing the activities. Introduce these words by beginning to use them yourself. Explain what you mean by them, but don't insist that students use them.

**Factor**   Ways of referring to the numbers that "work" in these activities can be wordy or cumbersome—"numbers you can count by to land exactly on 20," or "equal groupings that make 20." You can gradually introduce the word *factor*. If the introduction of a vocabulary word is preceded by activities that make its definition clear, students enjoy knowing an "adult" word to refer to a concept they have learned.

**Even and Odd**   These words will come up in the students' descriptions of patterns on the 100 chart. Don't assume that students know exactly what they mean by these words. When one teacher asked, "What do you mean by *even?*" to a child who was describing the pattern of 2's on the 100 chart, he provoked a 45-minute discussion about the characteristics of odd and even! Some children believe that an even number has only even factors: "No, 3 isn't a factor of 24 because 3 isn't even." This is a good conjecture to have students investigate.

**Row and Column**   In talking about their work with the 100 chart, students often confuse the words *row* and *column*, describing a pattern as going "down the row" rather than "down the column." This is a good opportunity to talk about the difference, since using *row* for both (as students often do) makes communication more difficult. However, do not insist that students use these words in the conventional way as long as they can explain or demonstrate what they mean. Remembering the difference can be hard, and focusing on getting the words right may obscure the good mathematical thinking a student is doing. Rather, keep using the terms yourself so that students continually hear them used correctly in context. Other terms that may come up in this context and may need some explanation are *horizontal*, *vertical*, and *diagonal*.

**Multiple**   You may want to hold off on this word until *factor* is well established in the classroom vocabulary, but it can be naturally introduced in Investigation 2, when students are dealing with multiples of 100: "Maya noticed that when we're counting by 25's, after every four numbers we get to a *multiple* of 100."

columns
↓

rows →

| 1 | 2 | 3 | 4 | 5 | 6 | 7 | 8 | 9 | 10 |
|---|---|---|---|---|---|---|---|---|---|
| 11 | 12 | 13 | 14 | 15 | 16 | 17 | 18 | 19 | 20 |
| 21 | 22 | 23 | 24 | 25 | 26 | 27 | 28 | 29 | 30 |
| 31 | 32 | 33 | 34 | 35 | 36 | 37 | 38 | 39 | 40 |
| 41 | 42 | 43 | 44 | 45 | 46 | 47 | 48 | 49 | 50 |
| 51 | 52 | 53 | 54 | 55 | 56 | 57 | 58 | 59 | 60 |
| 61 | 62 | 63 | 64 | 65 | 66 | 67 | 68 | 69 | 70 |
| 71 | 72 | 73 | 74 | 75 | 76 | 77 | 78 | 79 | 80 |
| 81 | 82 | 83 | 84 | 85 | 86 | 87 | 88 | 89 | 90 |
| 91 | 92 | 93 | 94 | 95 | 96 | 97 | 98 | 99 | 100 |

## Factors of 24, 36, and 48

In this discussion, related to the discussion activity on page 25, students are sharing the things they've discovered about the factors of 24, 36, and 48.

**Saloni:** I found a secret! If you do 24, you land right on 24!

**Does that work for other numbers?**

**Saloni:** Yes!

**Annie:** The number always works for itself, like 36 works for 36, and 48 works for 48.

**Sean:** The 3's worked on all of them.

**Tamara:** The 6's work for all of them, and the 2's work for all of them.

**Kate:** It's because they're all even numbers.

**Aaron:** Yeah, 2 will always work if it's even, 'cause counting by 2's is the even numbers.

**Maria:** If you can make 6's then you can make 3's, because I was doing it with the cubes, and I had 6's for 24, so then I just cut them in half, and then I had 3's.

**Sean:** And 9 always works when you have 3's.

**Kate:** I counted by 1's and it works on all of them.

**Ryan:** I agree with Kate. It doesn't matter what number, you can always count it by 1's.

**Latisha:** Wait, I don't think it's right what Sean said about the 9's. Nine doesn't work for 24.

**Sean:** It has to, because 3 does.

**Latisha:** No, because 9 and 9 is 18 and then another 9 would be too many.

**Ricardo:** Zero doesn't work.

**Why doesn't that work?**

**Ricardo:** Because you don't get anywhere!

From this discussion, the teacher recorded the following conjectures, which the class returned to throughout the unit as students worked with other factors and multiples:

- The number always works for itself.
- 2 will always work if it's even.
- If 6 is a factor, then 3 is a factor too.
- 1 is a factor of every number.
- 0 is never a factor.

Some teachers like to identify particular children as the authors of conjectures; for example, "Kate's conjecture—1 is a factor of every number."

❖ **Tip for the Linguistically Diverse Classroom**
Following the pattern established in the tip on page 22, include visual diagrams to support each conjecture. For example:

- 1 is a factor of every number.

- If 6 is a factor, then so is 3.

Provide opportunities for students who cannot articulate their conjectures to come to the board to present their ideas using similar visual illustrations.

# Factors of 100

## What Happens

Students find factors of 100. They make a set of 100 charts for the numbers that are factors of one hundred, skip counting by one factor on each chart. They make a design showing 100 things, grouped by one of the factors of 100. They make a second design, grouped by a different factor, at home. Their work focuses on:

- finding which numbers are factors of 100

- skip counting with the factors of 100

- figuring out how many of a certain factor make 100 (for example, that four 25's make 100)

 **Ten-Minute Math: Counting Around the Class** During the next few days, continue to do Counting Around the Class in short sessions outside of the mathematics hour.

Count by 4's or 5's. Before you begin, ask:

**Do you think our final number will be more than 100? Why do you think so?**

Stop two or three times during the count and ask questions like this:

**We're at 65 now—how many more students will have to have turns to reach 100?**

Some days, you might have students use a calculator for this activity. On most calculators, the equals (=) key allows you to skip count easily. For example, to skip count by 5's, press a starting number (typically, 0), the operation (in this case, +), and the number you want to count by (in this case, 5). Then, press the equals key each time you want to add 5. Thus, when you press

you will see on your screen 5, 10, 15, 20.

For full directions and variations on this activity, see p. 73.

## Materials

- Interlocking cubes
- Colored paper, scissors, glue or paste, crayons or markers, scrap materials
- Student Sheet 6 (2 per student)
- Student Sheet 7 (1 per student)
- Student Sheet 8 (1 per student, homework)

# What Numbers Are Factors of 100?

**Introducing "Landmark" Numbers** Briefly discuss the general idea of landmarks:

**What is a landmark? Why are they useful? Have you ever used landmarks, or seen anyone in your family use landmarks? Can a tree be a landmark? How about a building? Or a sign for a business?**

Explain that there are important numbers that we can use as "landmarks," to help us tell where we are when we are counting or figuring.

**When you count, do you get the feeling that some numbers are more important than others? If so, which ones? Why are these important?**

Students might suggest 2, 5, 10, 50, 100, or others. Explore their sense of these.

**When we reach a number like 10, or 50, or 100, it makes us feel comfortable—we know where we are. That's why we can think of numbers like these as "landmark numbers." The number 100 is a particularly important landmark in our number system. We're going to spend some time learning all about 100, as well as the other hundreds, which are all landmark numbers: 200, 300, 400, 500, 600, 700, 800, 900, 1000.**

**Ways to Make 100** Students work in pairs or small groups to find all the factors of 100. Give each student a copy of Student Sheet 6, Miniature 100 Charts, and Student Sheet 7, Factors of 100. (Although they work collaboratively, each student does his or her own recording.) For each factor of 100, a student marks a miniature 100 chart, counting by that number and recording how many "jumps" it took to reach 100. Interlocking cubes remain available for students who want to make equal groups to test whether a number is a factor of 100. (Students who have found factors of 100 in the Multiplication and Division unit, *Things That Come in Groups*, may move through this activity quickly.)

Let's try 65. Do you think it will work?

Well, no, because 65 plus 65 is more than 100—but let's try it to see.

Students use Student Sheet 7 to keep a list of every number they try, whether it does or does not "work" as a factor of 100. They also figure out how many of each factor makes 100 and record this information on Student Sheet 7. Students keep this work in their folders for reference throughout the unit. The miniature 100 charts might be cut out from Student Sheet 6 and made into a small book.

As you observe students working, pose questions for discussion:

**What did you find out so far? How do you know 3 doesn't work? How did you find out that 20 works? Were there any numbers that surprised you? Do you think you have all the factors of 100? Could there be any others? Why do you think so?**

❖ **Tip for the Linguistically Diverse Classroom** Ask students to communicate their thoughts through visual aids, as explained in the tip on page 28.

You will be following up on this activity in the next session by helping students make a class chart showing all the factors of 100 they found (see chart, p. 35).

**Activity**

## Making a Picture of 100

Students each make an arrangement that shows 100 of the same thing, coloring or pasting objects onto paper. Their 100 things should be arranged in groups—one of the factors of 100—so that someone looking at the picture could easily count the objects. For example, students might arrange their objects by 5's or by 10's—but let them choose their own groupings.

If students are drawing, encourage them to keep their pictures simple since they will have to draw a lot of them! Lay out any art or scrap materials on a table. Encourage students to be creative, using anything available in the classroom.

- Students have drawn pictures of 100 hearts or 100 balloons.
- Some students have used rubber stamps.
- One student made rubbings of the bumps on plastic building blocks.
- Another student made a collection of tiny strips of paper that she painstakingly cut out.
- One student wrote a list of 100 names.
- Another used a hole puncher to punch out 100 "holes" from colored paper, which he then glued onto another sheet.

# Sessions 4 and 5 Follow-Up

🏠 **Homework**

Students create a second arrangement of 100 at home, using a different factor. Directions are on Student Sheet 8, A Picture of 100. You may also want to send home sturdy, oversize paper for them to work on. Families are encouraged to participate in making the display with their child.

Avoid specific suggestions for what to use for the home chart; emphasize that students may use anything they want. Some students have used buttons, macaroni, paper clips, soda can pop-tops, popcorn kernels, toothpicks, dried beans, and rice grains. They can also draw pictures.

❖ **Tip for the Linguistically Diverse Classroom** Give students the chance to circulate around the class and look at the pictures of 100 their classmates made during the session, to help them understand the variations that are possible.

You might want to make a bulletin board display of the students' collections, with a heading something like "100 of Each."

**Note:** The class will discuss this work during the first session of Investigation 2; be sure to save their pictures for that discussion.

# What About Notation?

It is important that your students learn to recognize, interpret, and use the standard forms and symbols for multiplication and division, both on paper and on the calculator. In this unit, students will use these:

$$12 \atop \underline{\times 3}$$
  $$3 \times 12$$   $$12 \div 3$$   $$3\overline{)12}$$

Your challenge is to introduce these symbols in a way that allows students to interpret them meaningfully. That is, students must understand *what is being asked* in a problem that is written in standard notation. They can then devise their own way to find an answer. Notation is also useful as an efficient way to record a problem and its solution. It is not just a directive to carry out a particular procedure, or a signal to forget everything you ever knew about the relationships of the numbers in the problem!

Your students may come to you already believing that when they see a problem like $3\overline{)42}$, written in the familiar division format, they must carry out the traditional long-division procedure. Instead, we want them to use everything they know about these two numbers in order to solve the problem. They might skip count by 3's out loud or on the calculator. (For tips on skip counting on the calculator, see the Ten-Minute Math activity, p. 29.) Or they might use reasoning based on their understanding of number relationships:

> It takes ten 3's to make 30. Then there are three more 3's to get up to 39, that's thirteen 3's so far. Then 40, 41, 42—that's one more 3—it's 14!

> Well, half of 42 is 21, and I can divide 21 into seven groups of 3, so you double that, and it's 14.

Similarly, when students see a multiplication problem like $4 \times 55$ written vertically, they are likely to forget everything they know about these numbers and try to carry out multiplication with carrying. Instead, we want students to use what they know about landmarks in the number system and other familiar number relationships. For example:

> I know that two 50's make 100, and there's four 50's, so that's 200. Then I know that four 5's is 20, so it's 220.

Students need to get used to interpreting multiplication in both horizontal and vertical form as simply indicating a multiplication situation, not a particular way to carry out the problem. So, while you help students to read standard notation and to use it to record their work, keep the emphasis on understanding the problem context and using good number sense to solve the problem.

# Dividing a Dollar

## Materials

- Interlocking cubes
- 100 charts
- Sample coin collections in differing total amounts (48 to 60 cents), for each pair
- A container of coins for each small group (at least 50 pennies, 25 nickels, 12 dimes, 6 quarters)
- Student Sheet 9 (1 per student)

## What Happens

The class lists and discusses all the factors of 100 they have found. Students use coins to explore how to share a dollar equally among five people, then investigate ways to divide a dollar evenly among different numbers of people. Their work focuses on:

- continuing to explore which numbers are and are not factors of 100, using money as a context
- continuing to become familiar with how many of a certain factor make 100 (for example, that four 25's make 100), in the context of money
- determining the value of a collection of coins

 **Ten-Minute Math: Counting Around the Class** In short sessions at various times during the day, continue to do Counting Around the Class as described in Sessions 4 and 5. Try counting by 10's. For other variations, see page 73.

## Activity

### Listing the Factors of 100

Work with students to make a large class chart of all the factors of 100, based on their work in the preceding sessions. You'll need to make a chart that can remain posted. Have students help you list these factors from the least to the greatest. Ask:

**Do you think we have all the factors of 100? Why do you think so? Are there any numbers you didn't try that might work?**

Then add to the chart how many of each factor it takes to make 100, asking students to supply these numbers:

**How many 20's make 100? How do you know? Who can prove it a different way? How many 2's make 100? How do you know? Who has a different way to explain the solution?**

Encourage students to refer to their work with cubes and 100 charts as ways to explain what they think. For example:

> When I did it with cubes, we did it in 20's, and we needed 5 rows of 20's.

> I can tell it's five 20's because I counted on the 100 chart—20, 40, 60, 80, 100, that's five.

Add these results, with the associated words and multiplication equations, to your chart. Include only the factors your students have found.

| Factor of 100 | How many make 100? | Say it in words | Say it as an equation |
|---|---|---|---|
| 1 | 100 | 100 groups of 1 | $100 \times 1 = 100$ |
| 2 | 50 | 50 groups of 2 | $50 \times 2 = 100$ |
| 4 | 25 | 25 groups of 4 | $25 \times 4 = 100$ |
| 5 | 20 | 20 groups of 5 | $20 \times 5 = 100$ |
| 10 | 10 | 10 groups of 10 | $10 \times 10 = 100$ |
| 20 | 5 | 5 groups of 20 | $5 \times 20 = 100$ |
| 25 | 4 | 4 groups of 25 | $4 \times 25 = 100$ |
| 50 | 2 | 2 groups of 50 | $2 \times 50 = 100$ |
| 100 | 1 | 1 groups of 100 | $1 \times 100 = 100$ |

Ask students what they notice about the list. Someone may notice related pairs; for example, they may see 20 groups of 5 and 5 groups of 20 (or, two 50's and fifty 2's). If no student notices this, you might point out one of the matching pairs yourself. This discussion can lead students to identify factors that are not yet on their list. Those students who have already worked with arrays in the Multiplication and Division unit, *Things That Come in Groups*, may be able to describe why they think both pairs work.

If the chart is not yet complete, or if your students are not sure whether they have all the factors, tell them that you will keep the chart posted and add to it if they find more factors. You may also want to post miniature 100 charts showing the pattern for each factor.

## Working with Coins

Give pairs of students the small sample coin collections (a few pennies, nickels, dimes, and at least one quarter, in differing amounts from about 48 to 60 cents). Review the values of coins with your class:

**What is a nickel worth? A dime? A dime and a nickel together? How do you know? What is a quarter plus a nickel worth? How do you know? Which is the biggest coin? How much is it worth? Is the smallest coin worth the smallest amount of money?**

❖ **Tip for the Linguistically Diverse Classroom**   Reword questions so that students can respond nonverbally. For example:

**Show me a coin that is worth 5 cents.**

**Show me a coin that is worth 10 cents.**

**Show me two coins that equal 30 cents.**

Ask each pair to figure out how much money they have altogether. You may want to have each pair trade its coin collection with another pair and calculate the new total.

Have one pair tell how many of each coin is in their collection. Draw these on the board or put them on the overhead. Ask the class to come up with different counting strategies for figuring out the total.

**Note:** Each day you use money, students enjoy finding out how much their collection is worth before doing other activities. This provides for good practice in counting by 5's, 10's, and 25's. It also allows students to check their collection at the end of class to make sure they have the same total before putting their coins away.

## Dividing a Dollar Among Five People

**We're going to be finding out more about 100 by using money. If I had a dollar in pennies, how many pennies would I have?**

Establish that there are 100 pennies or 100 cents in a dollar.

**We're going to work on how we can split up 100 pennies evenly. If I had a dollar, could I share it equally between Midori and Chantelle? How much would each person get?**

Students will probably know how to divide a dollar in half. Hold a short discussion of how much each person would get and how the students know that. What coins could they use to make this amount?

Give each small group their container of additional coins, and pose the following problem for work in pairs or small groups:

**Now, could I split a dollar equally among Midori, Chantelle, Sean, Michael, and Khanh? How much would each person get? Find as many different ways as possible that you could divide a dollar equally among five people.**

In this activity, giving two dimes to each person is considered different from giving four nickels to each person. You can clarify this as you circulate. Once students have one solution, you can explain what a "different solution" is by saying something like this:

**Suppose you didn't have enough dimes to give everyone two dimes. Could you use some different coins to give each person an equal amount?**

**Recording and Sharing Solutions**   Students work in small groups, recording each way they find so that they can remember and report their solutions later. They might use pictures, words, symbols, or a combination of these. We have deliberately not provided a student sheet for recording their findings, so that students can devise their own way of recording their solutions. As you circulate, remind students to record each solution with words, numbers, or pictures.

Try to interpret their recording. If it is unclear, insist that they clarify:

**I can tell that you used nickels, but I don't understand how many nickels each person would get.**

After a while, have groups share their answers with the whole class. Ask each group to share a *new* method—one that has not yet been shown by someone else. To share their solution, they might specify in a sentence what each person gets, or they might arrange the coins on the overhead projector. You might want to keep a chart of their findings.

Your students may not realize at first that every solution they find involves giving 20 cents to each person. The **Dialogue Box**, Dividing a Dollar Among Five People (p. 40), illustrates how one pair discovered that they always had to use 20 cents.

# How Can We Divide a Dollar Evenly?

**Dividing a Dollar Among Three People**   Pose the following question to the whole class:

**Could you share a dollar equally among three people—Latisha, Mark, and Samir? How could you do it?**

There is a way, but it wouldn't be a fair way. Someone would have 34 cents and the rest 33 cents.

After sharing a dollar among two and five people, students may think that it is possible to split a dollar among any number of people. Trying to split a dollar among three people, however, will be puzzling to many.

One approach to this discussion is to put 10 towers of 10 cubes each on the overhead. Ask students what they would do to divide these "pennies" up among three people. See the **Dialogue Box**, 100 Cents and 3 People (p. 41), for part of a discussion that occurred in one classroom.

If this problem remains puzzling to some, leave it as an open question for students to continue exploring, working with coins or cubes in their groups.

**How Can You Split a Dollar Evenly?**   Review the class findings so far about how a dollar can be divided evenly. Start a class chart, as shown. Include numbers of people the students know cannot divide a dollar evenly.

Students may know some other numbers they can add to the chart; for example, that 10 people would each get 10 cents, or that 99 people cannot divide a dollar evenly. If students give such information, add it to the chart.

Students then work in pairs to find out what other numbers of people could share a dollar equally. Hand out Student Sheet 9, Ways to Split Up a Dollar, for their recording. To get students started, suggest that they choose one or two of the following to explore: 4 people, 8 people, 25 people, 50 people, or 30 people.

| Number of people sharing a dollar | How much each gets |
|---|---|
| 2 people | 50¢ |
| 5 people | 20¢ |
| | |

| Cannot split a dollar evenly |
|---|
| 3 people |

They may also choose other numbers that interest them. Some students will work on just one or two of these problems. Others may become interested in finding all the possible ways to divide a dollar evenly. In either case, it's important that each student be able to describe and justify his or her solutions.

Some students may come up with solutions that don't involve whole cents, for example, giving each of three people 33 1/3 cents. This is a good opportunity to talk about fractions of wholes and for the class to see and interpret fraction notation. Acknowledge that such an answer is an interesting mathematical solution, but that it would be impossible to actually give anyone 1/3 of a cent. Some students may be interested in recording these results on Student Sheet 9. You may also want to make a separate category for these on your class list: "Solutions that work with numbers, but not with pennies."

| Number of people sharing a dollar | How much each gets |
|---|---|
| 2 people | 50¢ |
| 5 people | 20¢ |
| 4 people | 25¢ |
| 20 people | 5¢ |
| 10 people | 10¢ |
| 100 people | 1¢ |

| Cannot split a dollar evenly |
|---|
| 3 people |
| 8 people |
| anything over 50 |

**Summing Up**   Add student findings to your class chart.

By this time, students should be quite familiar with the factors of 100. This is a good time to pause and make sure that your students are comfortable with the relationships between 100 and its factors, before you go on to work with higher numbers. Pose these two questions (write them on the board or overhead):

**Teacher Checkpoint**
# Factors of 100

> **How many 20's are in 100?**
> **How many 4's are in 100?**

Ask students to find the answers to these and to prove their solutions using coins, cubes, or 100 charts, then write or draw explanations of their solutions. The purpose of their writing and drawing is to demonstrate convincingly that their solution is correct. If you are keeping student portfolios, this piece of work could be one to save.

There may be some students who need more work with 100. When you go on to work with multiples of 100 in Investigation 2, you can adjust the numbers for those students. Thus, instead of finding how many 25's in 200 and 300, they might find how many 10's in 70, 80, and 90; how many 20's in 40, 60, and 80; and so forth.

There are 25 4's in 100.

I counted by 4 on the 100 chart.

I found 25 4's in a zig zag line.

# ▢D▢I▢A▢L▢O▢G▢U▢E▢ ▢B▢O▢X▢

## Dividing a Dollar Among Five People

This discussion between two students takes place while they are working together on the activity Dividing a Dollar Among Five People (p. 36).

**See how you could share a dollar equally among five people. I want you to find as many combinations as possible.**

[*Yoshi and Amanda are working together. Amanda lines up 5 dimes.*]

**Yoshi:** We found one—two dimes!

**Amanda:** Wait, I'm not sure yet. [*She adds a second dime on top of each of the first 5.*]

**Yoshi** [*impatiently*]: That's it!

**Amanda** [*not yet satisfied*]: We need to check it. Fifty plus fifty … yes.

**Yoshi** [*already onto another solution*]: They could each get 4 nickels … it's the same thing!

[*Amanda begins to try nickels, making piles of 4.*]

**Amanda:** I don't know if we've got enough to do it.

**Yoshi:** Yes, 4 nickels is the same thing. And we could use 20 pennies, it's the same thing. It works.

[*Amanda, working on a solution independently, places 1 dime and 2 nickels in each of five piles.*]

**Amanda** [*counting the dimes first*]: 10, 20, 30, 40, 50 … [*then the nickels*] 55, 60, 65, 70, 75, 80, 85, 90, 95, 100. [*She then tries groups of 5 nickels.*]

**Yoshi:** That's too many.

**Amanda:** No, wait, I want to try it! Don't worry, I know what I'm doing.

[*Amanda counts her nickels by fives. After the fourth pile, her count is already up to $1.00, with 5 nickels left, so she abandons this idea.*]

**Amanda:** Let's think of another one not using 20 cents. [*Pause.*] No, we have to use 20 cents, don't we?

**Yoshi:** We could do 10 pennies and 2 nickels, that would work.

[*Amanda again gets the coins to try it, as she is not convinced without using the coins.*]

# 100 Cents and 3 People

This class discussion takes place during the activity How Can We Divide a Dollar Evenly? (p. 38).

**Could you share a dollar equally among three people? How would you do it?**

**Elena:** 30 pennies.

**Dylan:** That equals 90.

*[The teacher puts three groups of 30 on the overhead.]*

**How about these 10 left over?**

**Ricardo:** I think you should put them in 20's.

*[The teacher puts out three groups of 20.]*

**Ricardo:** Give 10 to the 20's.

**Su-Mei:** It still equals 90.

**Aaron:** I don't see any way … I don't think you could do it.

**Yoshi:** 34.

**So keep these 30's and add 4 more to each? What do you think is going to happen then?**

**Latisha:** Two cents will get left over. You'll get 4 and 4 each and that's 8, and 8 from 10 is 2, so there's 2 left over.

**Sean:** I think 2's would work. No, do it by 1's.

**Jamal:** I think if you gave 33 each, you'd have one left over and you could divide it into thirds, if you had a butcher knife or something.

**Tamara:** It's impossible to divide 10 into three because 10 is an even number and 3 is an odd number, and you can't divide 10 into 3 equal groups.

**Aaron:** 33 plus 33 plus 33 equals 99, so how can you make 100?

**Ricardo:** I think if you take all those 30's and make 'em into 20's, it would work.

**Jennifer:** If you start with 5's, it might do it.

By the end of this discussion, some students believed that there is no solution with whole cents, while others were still convinced that sharing in the right way might make it possible to divide $1.00 in three ways evenly.

Students then worked with interlocking cubes to model this problem. Those who were pretty sure that there was no way to divide $1.00 evenly among three people enjoyed proving their solution with the cubes, while students who were unconvinced by the group discussion needed to work with the cubes themselves.

Tamara's conjecture, "You can't divide an even number by an odd number," is an idea that often comes up in this discussion. While Tamara is right that you can't divide 10 into three equal groups, her generalization does not hold up—for example, you can divide 10 by five. If this idea comes up in your class, you might want to list the conjecture somewhere, ask students to think about it, and discuss it further when students work on division problems later in the unit: "Can we ever divide an even number by an odd number? an odd number by an even number?"

# INVESTIGATION 2

# Using Landmarks to Solve Problems

## What Happens

**Sessions 1, 2, and 3: Moving Beyond 100**  After reviewing what they have found out about the factors of 100, students use this knowledge to explore larger numbers. Through a series of activities set up as choices, they explore the multiples of 100 with different tools, including money, the 300 chart, and the calculator. They solve problems involving multiplication and division by 20, 25, and other familiar factors, in the context of money. They examine the patterns in counting by 20's to 1000, and they begin to develop strategies for division using these patterns.

**Session 4: Solving Problems with Money**  After a whole-class discussion of one multiplication problem, students work in pairs on multiplication and division problems that involve money. They work carefully on one, two, or three problems, writing and drawing to explain how they found their solutions.

**Sessions 5 and 6: Real-World Multiplying and Dividing**  These sessions begin with an introduction to standard division notation. Students then apply their understanding of landmarks to multiplication and division problems in real-world contexts. Through a series of activities set up as choices, they solve given problems, find groups of objects in the classroom that are close to multiples of 100 (e.g., 30 students with 10 fingers each), and create and solve their own problems. They use multiplication and division notation to record their work, and learn to recognize a variety of symbols used to write down multiplication and division. They also become familiar with how to do multiplication and division on the calculator.

## Mathematical Emphasis

■ Using knowledge about factors of 100 to understand the structure of multiples of 100 (if there are four 25's in 100, there are twelve 25's in 300)

■ Developing strategies to solve problems in multiplication and division situations by using knowledge of factors and multiples

■ Estimating real quantities that are close to 200, 300, and 400

■ Reading and using standard multiplication and division notation to record

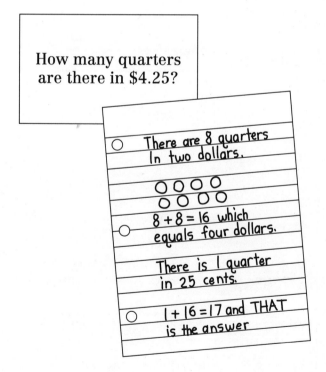

## What to Plan Ahead of Time

### Materials

- All materials used previously in the unit remain available: cubes, coins, and 100 charts. Make sure students know that they may use any of these materials that they would find helpful.
- Calculators: at least 1 per pair (all sessions)
- "Pictures of 100" that students made in Investigation 1 (Sessions 1–3)
- Overhead projector (Session 1)

### Other Preparation

- Duplicate student sheets and teaching resources (located at the end of this unit) in the following quantities:

*For all sessions*

300 chart (p. 94): 3–5 per student, and 1 overhead transparency

*For Sessions 1, 2, and 3*

Student Sheet 10, Exploring Multiples of 100: 1–2 per student

Student Sheet 11, Calculator Skip Counting: 1 per student

Money Problems (p. 95): 5 copies, cut apart, and sets placed in boxes or envelopes

*For Session 4*

More Money Problems (p. 96): 5 copies, cut apart, and sets placed in boxes or envelopes

*For Sessions 5 and 6*

Student Sheet 12, Multiplying Things in Class: 1 per student, or 1 to post for student reference

Division Problems (p. 97): 5 copies, cut apart, and sets placed in boxes or envelopes

# Moving Beyond 100

## Materials

- Students' pictures of 100
- Cubes, coins, and 100 charts
- Money Problems, in sets
- Student Sheet 10 (1–2 per student)
- Student Sheet 11 (1 per student)
- Transparency of 300 chart
- Overhead projector
- 300 chart (2–3 per student)

## What Happens

After reviewing what they have found out about the factors of 100, students use this knowledge to explore larger numbers. Through a series of activities set up as choices, they explore the multiples of 100 with different tools, including money, the 300 chart, and the calculator. They solve problems involving multiplication and division by 20, 25, and other familiar factors, in the context of money. They examine the patterns in counting by 20's to 1000, and they begin to develop strategies for division using these patterns. Their work focuses on:

- using what they know about 100 to think about multiples of 100
- proving how many groupings of a particular factor make 100

 **Ten-Minute Math: Calendar Math** Once or twice during the next few days, do Calendar Math. Remember, Ten-Minute Math activities are designed to be done outside of the math hour.

Ask students to give number combinations that equal the number of the day's date, using multiplication as part of their answer.

List student responses. For example, if the date is January 21, solutions could include $2 \times 10 + 1$, $3 \times 10 - 9$, or $5 \times 5 - 4$.

Choose a "favorite expression" for the day, perhaps the most unusual, or one that uses a new idea. Use this favorite to write the date on the board, for example: January $0 \times 21 + 21$.

For variations, see p. 75.

## Activity

### Hundreds from Home

**We've been working with the number 100 recently, and we're going to be working with even higher numbers soon. Let's start today by looking at the pictures of 100 you made earlier.**

Ask several students to show the arrangements of 100 objects or pictures they made at school and at home. Have them describe how they arranged the items to be able to "prove" that there are exactly 100 objects without counting them one by one.

Spend a bit of time adding by 100's, using the student displays as concrete objects to add. See the **Dialogue Box**, Hundreds from Home (p. 51), for an example. Ask questions such as:

**How many 20's are there altogether if we put Jamal's and Annie's together?**

**Four Choices** During Sessions 1–3 of this investigation, students may choose from four activities going on in the classroom simultaneously. This format allows students to explore the same idea at different paces. Some might try two activities during each hour mathematics class. They may repeat an activity, using different numbers or problems. They need not try all four choices.

**How to Set Up the Choices** If you set up your choices at stations, show students what they will find at each station. Otherwise, tell students where they can find the materials they need.

> Choice 1: Factors of Numbers Greater Than 100—copies of Student Sheet 10, cubes, and coins
>
> Choice 2: Money Problems—sets of Money Problems in boxes or envelopes
>
> Choice 3: Counting on the 300 Chart—copies of the 300 chart
>
> Choice 4: Calculator Skip Counting—calculators and copies of Student Sheet 11

Introduce the four activities. Choice 3, which involves the 300 chart, and Choice 4, which entails calculator skip counting, both need to be introduced with some whole-class work; see the following activity descriptions for specifics. (You may want to delay the introduction of Choice 4 until the beginning of Session 2.) Students then begin working on the activities of their choice.

You might list the four choices on the board, as a reminder for the students.

## Choice 1: Factors of Numbers Greater Than 100

Students take a copy of Student Sheet 10, Exploring Multiples of 100, along with cubes and coins for making groupings. Working alone or in pairs, students choose 4, 5, 10, 20, or 25 as a factor. They find out how many of their chosen number are in 100, how many are in 200, and how many are in 300.

Even if working in pairs, students fill out their own copies of Student Sheet 10. When completing the statement, "I know there are _____ in 300 because …," their sentence should have enough information to convince someone else how many of their factor are in 300. For examples of student work, see the illustration on page 47.

There is space on Student Sheet 10 for students to continue past 300 if they want. These students can complete the last section of Student Sheet 10, telling about any patterns they see. Some students may want to take a second student sheet and work on another factor after they have completed their work with the first.

### Choice 2: Money Problems

Students choose problems from the sets of Money Problems. They do not need to do all the problems; you can adjust your expectations for individual students. Students are to write about each problem on a separate piece of paper or in their mathematics notebook, telling how they solved it.

### Choice 3: Counting on the 300 Chart

Use the overhead transparency to introduce the 300 chart. Ask students to suggest one way to skip count on the chart that will land them exactly on 300. Ask how they know that number will work, and what they think the skip counting pattern for that number will look like on the chart. Mark the count for this number on the transparency as an example.

In this activity, students use copies of the 300 chart and find numbers that will land them exactly on 300 if they count by that number—in other words, they find factors of 300. They mark a 300 chart for each factor they find.

You may want to reread the **Teacher Note** in Investigation 1, Students' Problems with Skip Counting (p. 26); students may encounter similar problems in using the 300 chart.

### Choice 4: Calculator Skip Counting

Introduce calculator counting to the whole class. Ask students to contribute ideas about different ways to make the calculator skip count by 10's up to 300. (For basic instructions on making a calculator skip count, see the Ten-Minute Math activity on p. 29.) Give students some time to practice calculator skip counting by different numbers.

Make available copies of Student Sheet 11, Calculator Skip Counting. Students use the calculator to count by a number that will get them exactly to 300. Their task has three parts: to find a way to make the calculator count by this number, to keep track of how many of that number it takes to make 300, and to record their results on Student Sheet 11.

### While Students Are Working on the Choices

■ At some point during these three sessions, pause for the class discussion activity, Finding Patterns in the 20's (p. 47). Afterward, students may continue with the activities.

■ During Session 3, have each student spend some time on the Assessment activity (p. 48).

## Class Discussion: Finding Patterns in the 20's

Hold this discussion sometime during Sessions 1–3, after students have had time to try several of the activity choices. Choose a factor of 100 with which your students are quite comfortable. Using this factor, begin a chart, like this one for the factor 20.

| Number | How many 20's? |
|--------|----------------|
| 100    | 5              |
| 200    | 10             |
| 300    | 15             |

Ask students to look for patterns.

**What do you notice about the number of 20's as you look down the chart? How many 20's would there be in 400? How do you know?** [*Add this result to the chart.*] **Can you predict for higher numbers?** [*Add 500 and 600 to the chart.*]

**How many 20's are in 900? Why do you think so?** [*Pause on this question until many students have given their own explanations.*]

**How many 20's are in an "in-between" number, like 640? Does 20 work for 640? How do you know?**

This is an important discussion. Plan to spend about 20 minutes on it. See the **Dialogue Box**, How Many 20's in 280? (p. 52), for an example of a third grade discussion along these lines.

---

I know there are ___75 4's___ in 300 because  since there are 25 4's in 100, so I just counted it like quarters. And it came out 75.

I know there are ___30 10's___ in 300 because  10 plus 10 is 20, 20 plus 10 is 30.

I know there are ___fifteen 20's___ in 300 because  there are five in 100 so you add five three times, but we still used cubes to make sure.

I know there are ___60 5's___ in 300 because  I put a cube on the 300 chart after every 5, and then I counted them, and it was 20 for 100, 40 for 200, 60 for 300. But I also know another way because 20 and 20 and 20 is 60.

I know there are ___12 25's___ in 300 because  I know that in 3 dollars there are 12 quarters, so there must be 12 25's in 300.

---

*Typical student explanations of their reasoning on Student Sheet 10.*

## Assessment

## How Many in 500?

Toward the end of Sessions 1–3, ask students to work on another problem:

**How many 5's (or 20's, or 25's) are in 500?**

Since they don't have enough cubes or coins or counting chart squares to actually count to 500, they will need to use their knowledge about 100, 200, and 300 to visualize what happens as they go on to 400, then to 500.

You might assign different factors to different pairs of students; most should be working with 5, 20, or 25. Students who do not seem ready for this assignment could find the number of 10's in 500. Students needing a more difficult challenge can find how many 4's are in 500.

When pairs of students are finished, ask them to write down their solution or to explain their solution to you. Tell them you will be looking at everyone's solution. Because some students may not be adept at conveying their thinking in writing, it is important that you spend enough time with every individual to assess their strengths and needs.

Use these questions to guide your observation and questioning, both during this assessment and during their other work in Sessions 1–3:

- Are students able to skip count confidently, knowing where to start, and making use of visual or numerical patterns to insure accuracy?
- Do they make appropriate use of tools (coins, cubes, counting charts) to solve these problems?
- Can they build on partial solutions (such as their knowledge of the number of 5's in 100) to develop solutions for higher numbers (the number of 5's in 500)?
- Do they notice and correct their own mistakes? Do they double-check their counting strategies?

Refer to the **Teacher Note**, Assessment: How Many in 500? (p. 49), for commentary on some sample student responses.

## Sessions 1, 2, and 3 Follow-Up

 **Homework**

- Students can take home Money Problems they have not yet done (from the class sets), or similar problems that you create.
- They might take their 300 chart home to look for other numbers that land exactly on 300 when they skip count by that number.

■ Another homework problem:

**How many 4's are there in 600?**

Students must write a sentence to show how they figured it out, and draw a picture to explain their answer to another student. You can adjust the difficulty level of this problem for various students. Counting by 4's is harder than 5's or 25's, and 10's is easier than any of these.

---

# Assessment: How Many in 500?

The assessment question, "How many 5's (or 20's, or 25's) are in 500?" is a difficult problem for many students, and you may not see many perfect solutions. However, students' approaches to the problem will give you a great deal of information about their familiarity with the factors of 100, their facility with skip counting, and their understanding of the relationship between 100 and its multiples. The following examples of student responses demonstrate the process.

### Maria: How Many 20's in 500?

To explain her answer, 25, Maria writes:

> There are 5 20's in 100, so do it 5 times and it's 25.

**Can you explain it a little more?**

Maria: It's easy. You know there are five 20's in 100.

**How do you know?**

Maria: Because [*showing one finger for each number she counts*], 20, 40, 60, 80, 100. See, five twenties. Then, it's just the same for 200, so it's five more, then five more for 300, until you get to 500. That's 5, 10, 15, 20, 25 [*again, she shows one finger for each count*].

The teacher wants to see whether Maria can use this method with other numbers.

**What would happen for 5's? How many 5's in 500? How could you do it?**

Maria: Well, you'd do the same thing. Find out how many in 100, then just count that 5 times.

**Do you know how many are in 100?**

Maria [*thinks for a minute*]: Um, I'm not sure, but I could figure it out if I counted by 5's.

Maria is comfortable with skip counting by 20's and with using the method of skip counting to find out how many of a particular number are in some multiple of that number. She is able to keep track of her work; she "double counts" easily—that is, she counts by 20's while also keeping track of the number of 20's she is counting. She has a clear grasp of how 100 is related to its multiples, and she can use this information to solve problems. However, she does not see that her knowledge that there are five 20's in 100 gives her information about how many 5's are in 100.

### Aaron and Ricardo: How Many 4's in 500?

The teacher gives Aaron and Ricardo this slightly more difficult problem, having already seen them solve quite easily the problem that Maria worked on. The two students decide that there are 204 fours in 500. They use the 100 chart and explain their solution this way:

> See, we counted by 4's and got 28, and then we doubled it and got 56, and then we got 102, and then 204!

*Continued on next page*

From their work and some further questioning, the teacher notices that they have good strategies for adding numbers, and that they understand how to skip count in order to figure out how many of a number are in one of its multiples. However, they have difficulty keeping track of their count, and when they make an error in counting, they don't catch it.

This is a pattern the teacher has noticed in Aaron and Ricardo's work—some elegant strategies that are undermined by small errors and a lack of checking. The teacher makes a mental note to emphasize the use of more than one strategy to help Aaron and Ricardo double-check their work. Then the teacher asks them how they know they have the correct number of 4's for 100. When they say, "We counted," the teacher asks if they could use the pattern on their 100 chart to see if they counted correctly.

### Tamara and Jamal: How Many 20's in 500?

This pair of students at first seem baffled by the problem. They have a hard time getting started, and when the teacher asks them what they are thinking, Tamara says, "We can't do it. We don't have enough blocks." The teacher asks them to figure out how many 20's are in 100, and the two set to work building.

First they count out 100 cubes, then begin taking groups of 20, counting by 1's. Then the teacher comes around to their workspace again, asking "Is there any way you can make your 20's by counting by a bigger number?" Jamal replies, "By 10's!"

Since many of the interlocking cubes are already put together in groups of 10, the two students quickly assemble groups of 20's. They count the groups of 20's by 10's until they get to 100, and write down on their paper:

There are 5 20's in 100. This is how we know. We have 20 + 20 + 20 + 20 + 20 and that makes 100.

The teacher asks them to find the number of 20's in 200, and they use the same method, making 20's until they reach 200, counting by 10's to make sure they have exactly 200, then counting the number of groups of 20.

Tamara and Jamal need a lot more experience with counting by 10's and 20's and answering questions about 100, 200, and 300. They are comfortable building with cubes, but need to do more counting on the 300 chart as they construct their cube groups, so that they begin to associate the numerical patterns with the groups they are counting. They need to become comfortable counting by numbers larger than 10 and to see how the things they do in the first hundred can help them with what happens in the next hundred.

## Hundreds from Home

In this discussion during the first session of Investigation 2 (p. 44), the class is talking about the pictures of 100 the students made at home.

**What did Ryan do here that's extra-special?** [*Ryan has glued 100 metal soda can pop-tops onto a piece of cardboard.*]

**Chantelle:** He recycled.

**That's what I was thinking too. How did you arrange them, Ryan?**

**Ryan:** I did them by 10's. We have tons of them at home.

**Look at this display of popcorn kernels, 10 by 10. What could we call that?**

**Seung:** Rows and columns.

**Dominic:** It's like a 100 chart.

**Yes, it's very organized. Dominic, tell me about your display.**

**Dominic:** I cut out little squares and I put them by 5's in an X, the way the five is on dice.

**Laurie Jo did her stamps in 5's also. How did you arrange them?**

**Laurie Jo:** I have 20 rows of 5's, and that makes 100.

**If we put Dominic's and Laurie Jo's charts together, what we would have?**

**Ricardo:** 200!

**Jamal:** There would be twenty 5's.

**Su-Mei:** Ten 5's make 100, so twenty 5's for 200.

**If we put the popcorn with the pop-tops, what would we get?**

**Jeremy:** 200.

**And if we put these macaroni pieces with them?**

**Yvonne:** 300.

[*The teacher points to two student displays made from 100 bits of cut-up paper.*]

**What if we put this big batch of paper with this other big batch?**

**Annie:** 200.

**And what if we put everyone's 100's together?**

**Elena:** Twenty-one hundred?

**Why do you think that?**

**Elena:** Because there are 22 people, and everybody brought something but Mark. And everybody had one hundred.

**What does anyone else think?**

**Ly Dinh:** I think you could count by 100. It would be ten, then ten more, and one extra, so it would be twenty-one hundred.

**Is there any other name for twenty-one hundred?**

**Chantelle:** Twenty hundred and one?

**Mark:** Two thousand and one.

**Michael:** Two thousand and one hundred.

At this point, this teacher chose to list all these ideas about naming this number on a piece of chart paper to return to later during the last investigation in this unit.

## How Many 20's in 280?

A third grade class has created a class chart to show how many 20's are in multiples of 100, as explained in the activity Finding Patterns in the 20's (p. 47). Here they are discussing patterns in their chart.

| Number | How many 20's? |
|--------|----------------|
| 100 | 5 |
| 200 | 10 |
| 300 | 15 |
| 400 | 20 |
| 500 | 25 |
| 600 | 30 |
| 700 | 35 |
| 800 | 40 |
| 900 | 45 |
| 1000 | 50 |

**What if we listed an in-between number, like 640? First we have to decide, is 640 a multiple of 20?**

**Students** [*variously*]: Yes … No … Yes …

**Michael:** Because 20 + 20 is 40, and 600 has 30 twenties in it.

**Rashad:** What did he say?

**Michael:** Because we already know that every 100 has 5 twenties, so that's up to 600. Then you just count by 20's—20, 40—and you get to 640.

**What about 710?**

**Jennifer:** I think it's the same thing. You can do 20's to 700, and then … oh, I don't know.

**Su-Mei:** Just see if 10 is a multiple of 20. [*She checks on her miniature 100 chart on which she counted by 20's.*] Because 10 is BEFORE 20, so there's no way it could be a multiple.

**How about 360? Is it a multiple of 20?**

**Ryan:** Yes, because if you count by 20 you land on 60.

Sensing that some of the students are not following this discussion as well as the more vocal ones, the teacher asks everyone to think about how many 20's are in 280. The students are encouraged to talk among themselves. After a few minutes, the teacher asks for their solutions.

**Amanda:** Four 20's represents 80, and there are ten 20s in 200. Then you add 10 + 4, and it's 14.

**Tyrell:** I used the chart. So there were ten 20's in 200. Then I counted 20, 40, 60, 80.

**Midori:** I drew some boxes to represent 20's. I just guessed at how many there were at first. Then I skip counted each box by 20's. Then when I got to 280, I stopped and counted the boxes.

**Jennifer:** Seung helped me. First I told her that four 20's make 80. Then she asked me how many 20's were in 100 and I told her 5. Then she asked how many in 200 and I knew it was 10. So I added it and got 14.

**Saloni:** I counted on my fingers how many 20's in 100, and there were 5, and I knew there were four 20's in 80, and I added them.

**Liliana:** I drew five 20's and it went 20, 20, 20, 20, 20. And every time I got five, I put a circle and wrote how much it was worth, and I got 14.

# Solving Problems with Money

## What Happens

After a whole-class discussion of one multiplication problem, students work in pairs on multiplication and division problems that involve money. They work carefully on one, two, or three problems, writing and drawing to explain how they found their solutions. Their work focuses on:

- using their knowledge of factors to solve problems in multiplication and division situations
- recording their solutions in a way that explains their thinking to others

🕐 **Ten-Minute Math: Calendar Math**  Once or twice during the next few days, continue to do Calendar Math. This is a good activity to start the school day. Ask students to give number combinations that equal the number of the day's date, this time using division as part of their answer. For example, if the date is January 21, solutions could include $100 \div 5 + 1$, $100 \div 100 + 20$, or $50 \div 2 - 4$. List student responses. For full directions and variations, see p. 75.

## Materials

- Cubes, coins
- 100 charts, 300 charts
- More Money Problems, in sets

---

**Activity**

## Class Discussion: Six People Paying $1.50 Each

Pose the following problem :

> At a certain school, lunch costs $1.50. If six people buy lunch one day, how much money will the teacher have after collecting their money?

Or, use other familiar real-world situations: at a museum, admission is $1.50; bus fare is $1.50; and so forth.

**Note:** Always feel free to substitute or add problems from real-world contexts familiar to your students. Many of the problems in this unit were invented by teachers, based on situations familiar to their students.

Give students a few minutes to talk among themselves or to jot down or sketch a solution. Then ask them to share their strategies. Encourage students to share the way they started, even if they didn't fully solve the problem. See the **Dialogue Box**, Six People with $1.50 Each (p. 55).

## Problems Using Money

Make available the sets of More Money Problems, in boxes or envelopes. Students choose one, two, or three of these problems or similar problems you have created. If you create your own, include a mixture of multiplication and division situations. You may want to modify the given problems, using larger or smaller numbers, to meet the needs of individual students.

Students can work in pairs to solve the problems, but each student records the solution for each problem. Some pairs of students will require a whole session to do one problem. Encourage them to use cubes, coins, or 300 charts.

The point of doing only a few problems is to give students time to work out their solutions, double-check them, and write or draw to describe how they got each solution. Students are expected to find their own ways of recording their work on a plain sheet of paper. As you interact with students, make sure you can understand their sketch or explanation; if you can't, ask them to revise it to make it clearer.

## Session 4 Follow-Up

 **Homework**

Give students an additional problem from the sets of More Money Problems, to do as homework.

# Six People with $1.50 Each

This discussion occurred after students had worked on the money problem posed in the activity on p. 53.

**How did you figure out how much $1.50 lunch money, collected from six people, is altogether?**

**Liliana:** I put two lunches together, then I added—$3.00, $6.00, $9.00.

**Who did it a different way?**

**Cesar:** I drew 6 lines.

**What did they represent?**

**Cesar:** One dollar, so that was 6 dollars. And then I put six 50's and kept adding two 50's to make more dollars. I got 3 dollars and added them to the 6 dollars I had.

**Amanda:** I had $6.00, then I went [*holding up a finger for each 50 cents*] $6.50, $7.00, $7.50, $8.00, $8.50, $9.00.

**Dylan:** I had 6 dollars, one dollar for each $1.50. Then I know that if I had 4 more dollars, it would be 10. But 6 more 50 cents's only makes 3 dollars, so that's one less than 4, so it's 9.

**Khanh:** On my paper I put 6 lines for 50's and then circled groups of dollars and added them on to 6.

**Jennifer:** I drew 50 cent pieces and said two 50's is $1.00 and so on, and I came up with $9.00.

# Real-World Multiplying and Dividing

## Materials

- More Money Problems, in sets
- Coins, cubes, 300 charts
- Calculators
- Student Sheet 12 (1 per student, or 1 posted)
- Division Problems, in sets

## What Happens

These sessions begin with an introduction to standard division notation. Students then apply their understanding of landmarks to multiplication and division problems in real-world contexts. Through a series of activities set up as choices, they solve given problems, find groups of objects in the classroom that are close to multiples of 100 (e.g., 30 students with 10 fingers each), and create and solve their own problems. They use multiplication and division notation to record their work, and learn to recognize a variety of symbols used to write down multiplication and division. They also become familiar with how to do multiplication and division on the calculator. Their work focuses on:

- developing their own strategies to solve problems, using their knowledge of factors and multiples
- using standard multiplication and division notation to record work
- using the calculator to do multiplication and division problems

 **Ten-Minute Math: Calendar Math**  Continue using Calendar Math in short sessions outside the mathematics hour. Ask for combinations that involve division, as described in Session 4. Consider having students work individually or in pairs with calculators as they look for new ways to make the day's date. For full directions and variations, see p. 75.

see p. 75.

---

## Activity

### Using Standard Notation for Division

Pose a division problem in words, based on a real situation that is familiar to your students. Keep the numbers small and familiar, and don't tell your students that this is division. Here are some examples you can use or modify:

Suppose I'm building toy cars. I bought a box of 24 little wheels to use on the cars. How many cars could I build with the 24 wheels?

I'm going to share a little snack-size box of raisins among three people—myself and two friends. I counted the raisins in the box and found out there are exactly 30 raisins. How many can each person have?

Suppose I wanted to divide this class into two teams. How many would be on each team?

Start with one problem. Ask students to solve it and briefly explain their solutions. You may want to encourage the use of cubes for a concrete representation of the problem.

Then ask if the students know some ways to write the problem down, without its solution, using numbers and symbols. Have everyone try to write down one way. Reread the **Teacher Note**, What About Notation? (p. 33), for more about the relationship between student strategies and standard notation.

Write the problem on the board in words, and then record student suggestions for how to use the symbols. You may end up with many different ways, some of which are correct and some of which are not.

How many cars can I make with 24 wheels ?

$$4 \div 24$$

$$24 \div 4$$

$$4\overline{)24}$$

$$24\overline{)4}$$

Acknowledge that writing down division is very confusing. Show the two correct ways of writing the problem, and then show how to record the solution each way.

$$24 \div 4 = 6 \qquad\qquad 4\overline{)24}^{\,6}$$

Point out that these two different forms can be hard to remember because they are read in different directions, and the numbers are in different places. Ask students to describe the differences between the two notations, and ask them if they have any ideas about how they can remember how to write each one. For more about division notation, see the **Teacher Note**, Talking and Writing about Division (p. 62).

Try another problem or two. Have students solve the problem and then write down the problem and solution using numbers and division symbols. They will have the chance to practice using standard notation for recording during the next few activities.

**Note:** Some students may also use the fractional forms of recording division:

$$^{24}\!/_4 \qquad \frac{24}{4}$$

Acknowledge those as correct, but focus on the other two forms for now.

# Choice Time: Working with Landmarks

**Four Choices**   During Sessions 5–6 of this investigation, students may choose from four activities going on in the classroom simultaneously. This flexible format allows students to explore the same idea at different paces. Students may try all or just some of the activities, and they may repeat those that work best for them, using different numbers or problems.

**How to Set Up the Choices**   After introducing standard notation for division with the preceding activity, introduce the four activities students may choose from for the remainder of Session 5 and Session 6. If you set up your choices at stations, show students what they will find at each station. Otherwise, tell students where to get what they need for each choice.

> Choice 1: More Money Problems—sets of More Money Problems in boxes or envelopes
>
> Choice 2: Multiplying Things in Class—copies of Student Sheet 12 (or 1 copy, posted)
>
> Choice 3: Division Problems—sets of Division Problems in boxes or envelopes
>
> Choice 4: Making Up Landmark Problems—paper and pencils

In all four activities, encourage students to use their knowledge of factors and multiples to solve the problems.

You might list the four choices on the board, as a reminder for the students.

## Choice 1: More Money Problems

Students continue to work on problems they have not yet solved from the sets of More Money Problems. They may use cubes or coins if they want.

## Choice 2: Multiplying Things in Class

Instructions for this activity are given on Student Sheet 12, Multiplying Things in Class. Make copies available, or simply read and post the sheet. The goal is to find and count large numbers of things in the classroom that come in groups, such as fingers, boxes of crayons, chair legs, or floor tiles. Students can record individually what they find. Or, you can make a class list of what they find and how many there are of each thing.

If you have packages with the same number of items in each box (for example, paper clips), you might want to put them out for students to find. Students could also add things from another room to their count; for example, the number of chair legs in two classrooms.  For different approaches students may take, see the **Teacher Note**, Using Multiples to Count (p. 61).

**Note:** In this activity, some students may be ready to use their knowledge of landmark numbers to reason about numbers that are close to these landmarks. For example, consider the problem, "How many playing cards are there in three decks?" The number 52 (cards per deck) is close to the landmark number 50. So, students might combine their knowledge of counting by 50's with their knowledge of counting by 2's to solve the problem $52 \times 3$. For an example of one student's experience with near-landmark numbers, see the **Dialogue Box**, How Many Teeth in Our Class? (p. 63).

## Choice 3: Division Problems

Students work on one or two of the problems from the Division Problems sets and record with words or pictures, on another sheet of paper, how they solved the problem. They also write the problem and solution using standard division notation.

You can make up additional problems to provide an appropriate level of challenge for individual students. Some students may need more practice with problems involving familiar factors (20, 25, 5, and so forth), while others can begin to branch out to problems involving less familiar factors (for example, 15 or 30).

## Choice 4: Making Up Landmark Problems

Students make up their own problems, like the ones they've been working on, and illustrate them. You might establish three rules:

1. Each problem must use important landmark numbers, like 20's, 25's, 75's, 100's, and so forth.
2. Each problem must be a real, or at least realistic, situation.
3. You must solve every problem you write. Use a separate piece of paper for the solution.

Students enjoy having their problems (without the solutions) put together into a class book. This book can be sent home and can be used for additional practice.

**While Students Are Working on the Choices**  At some point during these two sessions, interrupt student work for the following:

- Share and discuss some of the multiplication problems students have created from things in the classroom (Choice 2). What did they find? How did they count the items?
- Do the activity Multiplying and Dividing on the Calculator (p. 60) with the whole class or small groups.

## Multiplying and Dividing on the Calculator

Sometime during these two sessions, encourage students to try some simple multiplication and division problems on the calculator. If you have enough calculators, you can do this with the whole class. Students can work with calculators individually or in pairs, taking turns pressing the keys. Otherwise, you can do this with smaller groups as students are working on other choices.

Pose a real-world problem, using small and familiar numbers (such as the toy car problem suggested earlier). Ask students to solve this on their calculator.

**What keys did you need to press to solve the problem? Are the symbols on the calculator similar to the standard notation for multiplication and division? Is the order in which you press calculator keys similar to the way you write down a problem?**

If you have a variety of calculators in the classroom, students can compare them to see if they work in the same way.

## Sessions 5 and 6 Follow-Up

**Homework**

- Choice 2, Multiplying Things in Class (Student Sheet 12), can be adapted for homework. Ask students to look for large numbers of things at home, record what they find, and describe how they figured the total.
- Choice 4, Making Up Landmark Problems, can also be continued as homework.

I have 300 peanuts in a bag and 25 kids in my class. How can I split the peanuts so we all get the same?

■ **Things That Number in the Low Hundreds** Once students have had some experience with things that number close to 200, 300, or 400, they might be able to predict other things found in these quantities around the school, the neighborhood, or at home. Make a list of students' ideas. Give them some time (either during class or as homework) to count the things in order to verify their ideas. If you started a class list of the quantities students found in the Choice 2 activity, you can now add the other things they find.

■ **Things That Number in the High Hundreds** Ask students to think of (or find) things that number close to even greater multiples of 100. That is, what can they think of that might be counted as 500? 700? 1000? This search is also a good opportunity to involve students' families: Find things at home that total close to 500. This work will connect to activities in Investigation 3 of this unit.

■ **Exploring Different Calculators** Ask students to explore any calculators they may find at home. Are the symbols the same as those on the ones they use in school? Can they do multiplication and division problems the same way? Students might draw a picture of any calculator that looks different to them and share these differences with the class.

---

## *Using Multiples to Count*

 **Teacher Note**

In these sessions, students find examples of things that give them a chance to visualize 100, 200, and 300, and that let them explore ways they can figure out multiplication situations such as "30 chairs, with 4 legs each." There are several good ways to count the legs of 30 chairs.

■ Some students may note that there are 25 fours in 100 and then 5 more fours, making 120.

■ Others might use the 100 or 300 charts to skip count by four 30 times.

■ Some might count by four 10 times, getting to 40, then add 40 three times on the calculator.

Encourage students who are only counting by 1's to begin to take some shortcuts, based on what they know about skip counting from previous sessions.

Various division symbols are used as standard notation in our society:

$$24 \div 4 \qquad 4\overline{)24} \qquad {}^{24}\!/_4 \qquad \frac{24}{4}$$

There are also different ways to "read" or speak of these notations:

1. Four goes into (or, as students say, "guzinta") 24

2. 24 divided by 4

3. How many 4's are in 24?

4. When 24 is shared among 4 people, how many does each person get?

So many symbols and so many different ways of reading them can be very confusing to young students. Especially confusing is the fact that the numbers and symbols appear in different positions, depending on the notation you are using.

In this unit, we ask students to recognize only the first two forms of notation. The first two ways of "reading" these notations correspond to the ways the symbols are written, and may seem simpler to you. However, "goes into" does not convey any mathematical meaning, and "divided by" may not be easily understood by students who don't yet understand what division is. The third and fourth ways of speaking carry more meaning for young students.

In this unit, we want to focus on the "grouping" interpretation of division: "How many 4's are in 24?" If students learn to read the two standard notations in this way, they will more likely attach meaning to the numbers and symbols.

For more about helping students connect their own good strategies with standard notation, see the **Teacher Note**, What About Notation? (p. 33).

# How Many Teeth in Our Class?

Mark, a third grader, is doing Choice 2: Multiplying Things in Class (p. 58). He has decided to figure out how many teeth there are in the classroom. Mark comes to his teacher with his paper showing a long column of 24's.

**Mark:** I know that I have 24 teeth, and so I figured that everyone in my class is about my age, so they probably have about 24 teeth too. But I don't know how to add it up.

**Would it help if you thought of the 24's as 25?**

**Mark:** Oh! Well, four 25's is 100, so four 24's is, let's see, it's one less for each one ... 96! [*Mark then groups his nineteen 24's into groups of four and writes 96 + 96 + 96 + 96 + 62.*]

**Where did the 62 come from?**

**Mark:** Well, I had three 24's left over, and that's 20, 40, 60—whoops!—that's 72, not 62.

**Is there a way you can think of those 96's so that they are easier to add—just like you thought of the 24's as 25's?**

**Mark:** They could be 100's—then I would just have to subtract four from each 100. That's 400 take away 16, so that's, let's see, take away 20 is 380, um ... 384. [*Mark then adds 384 and 72 on the calculator, and says excitedly*] 456! That's a lot of teeth!

# Constructing a 1000 Chart

## What Happens

**Session 1: A 1000 Chart** Students construct a poster-size chart of 1000 centimeter squares. Each pair constructs their 1000 out of a particular factor of 1000—either 20, 25, or 50—and labels each group up to 1000.

**Sessions 2 and 3: Finding Large Quantities** Students identify items that are found in large quantities in school or at home and relate those quantities to numbers on their 1000 chart. They then use the 1000 charts to calculate the "distance" (the difference) between numbers such as 550 and 950.

## Mathematical Emphasis

- Using factors of 100 to understand the structure of 1000 (how many 50's does it take to make 1000?)

- Estimating quantities up to 1000 (what can we find in the classroom that numbers about 500?)

- Using landmarks to calculate "distances" within 1000 (how far is it from 650 to 950?)

## What to Plan Ahead of Time

### Materials

- Large poster or chart paper: 1 sheet per pair  (Session 1)
- Scissors (Session 1)
- Glue or tape (Session 1)
- Crayons or markers (Session 1)
- Small counters or cubes, 1 cm or less: 1 per student (Sessions 2–3)
- String or ribbon (Sessions 2–3, optional)
- All materials used previously in the unit remain available: cubes, coins, 100 charts, 300 charts, calculators. Encourage students to use any of these materials that they would find helpful.

### Other Preparation

- Duplicate one-centimeter graph paper: 3–4 sheets per pair (or enough to give them 1000 squares, with extra for waste and experimentation) (Session 1)
- Construct a larger classroom 1000 chart with squares grouped by 20's or 25's and carefully sequenced. Use squares that are at least 1 inch or 2 centimeters on a side. Print the number for each block of squares (20, 40, 80 ..., or 25, 50, 75 ...) in the lower right square of the block. (Sessions 2–3, optional)

# A 1000 Chart

## What Happens

**Materials**

- One-centimeter graph paper (3–4 sheets per pair)
- Large poster or chart paper (1 sheet per pair)
- Scissors
- Glue or tape
- Crayons or markers
- Cubes, coins, 100 charts, 300 charts, calculators

Students construct a poster-size chart of 1000 centimeter squares. Each pair constructs their 1000 out of a particular factor of 1000—either 20, 25, or 50—and labels each group up to 1000. Their work focuses on:

- Counting to 1000 by one of its factors
- Keeping track of how many groups are needed to make 1000
- Organizing and labeling groups clearly so that any number on the 1000 chart can be located easily

 **Ten-Minute Math: Counting Around the Class**  Once or twice during the next few days, outside of math class, return to the short activity Counting Around the Class.

Try counting by 20's or 25's. Stop two or three times during the count and ask questions like this:

**We're at 450 now—how many students have we counted?**

After the count is complete, ask further questions:

**If we keep going, so that everyone has a second turn, how many students will have to have a second turn so that we reach 1000?**

For full directions and variations on this activity, see p. 73.

---

## Activity

### Making a Thousand

Give brief directions for this task: Each pair of students must cut out from the one-centimeter graph paper exactly 1000 squares and glue or tape them to the large sheet of poster or chart paper, to make a 1000 chart.

They can cut their squares out in groups of 20's, 25's, or 50's. That is, a pair who decides to make their chart by 25's will need to cut out 40 blocks of 25 one-centimeter squares, paste them to the large chart paper, and number each block—25, 50, 75, 100, 125, … up to 1000.

If students ask, "How many squares are on the graph paper?" or "How many 20's will I need?" tell them that part of their job is to answer these questions for themselves. Let students figure out for themselves how to arrange their blocks of squares on the large paper, but remind them that they must arrange the squares so that someone looking at their chart could easily count the groups. They should be able to convince someone else that there are exactly 1000 squares on their chart when it is finished.

Third graders need about a one-hour class session to complete and label their chart. Some students may start labeling each group of 25 squares with 25, 25, 25 ... instead of 25, 50, 75.... Make sure they understand that they are to label each block of squares with the total so far, not just with the number they are counting by.

Circulate as students are working, asking questions that will push them to think mathematically about the process they are following. For example:

**How many squares do you have? How many more do you need? How many more 20's (25's, 50's) do you need?**

Ask pairs of students to review each others' 1000 charts to help correct misplaced numbers and to see if they can find numbers easily on each others' charts. If some students finish early, they can challenge each other to locate particular numbers on their charts (see Locating Numbers on the 1000 Chart, the first activity in Sessions 2 and 3).

## Session 1 Follow-Up

Challenge students to find a quantity of something at home that matches one (or more) of the numbers on their 1000 chart that's greater than 300. Students should record what they find for use in the activities in Sessions 2 and 3.

 **Homework**

# Finding Large Quantities

## Materials

- Students' 1000 charts
- Small counters
- String or ribbon (optional)
- The large 1000 chart you made (optional)

## What Happens

Students identify items that are found in large quantities in school or at home and relate those quantities to numbers on their 1000 chart. They then use the 1000 charts to calculate the "distance" (the difference) between numbers such as 550 and 950. Their work focuses on:

- locating numbers between 1 and 1000
- estimating and counting real quantities up to 1000
- finding differences between two numbers by skip counting

 **Ten-Minute Math: Counting Around the Class** Continue to do Counting Around the Class at different times during the class day, as described in Session 1. Now that students are working with larger numbers, you might try counting by 50's or 100's. For other variations, see p. 73.

For other variations, see p. 73.

## Activity

### Locating Numbers on the 1000 Chart

Using the 1000 charts made in Session 1, ask students to locate particular numbers. Students should each have a small counter, piece of paper, or centimeter cube to place on their charts as you call a number.

For example, you might call "200." Students place their counters on 200 (or simply point to it) on their charts. You can circulate around the room quickly to check on students' accuracy and help those who are having difficulty.

At first, call out only multiples of 100. As students become more confident, call out multiples of the factors they have used—520, 375, 950, and so forth. Finally, call out any numbers up to 1000, such as 201, 335, 549, 857. Ask students to take turns picking numbers for the rest of the class to locate on their charts.

Repeat this activity several times during these two sessions. (One approach is to both start and end both sessions with this activity.) You may want to use the larger 1000 chart with the whole class or with small groups of students, especially if some of the students' charts aren't well organized.

Working in pairs, students try to find quantities of five to ten different items in the school that can be matched with numbers on the 1000 chart. For example, students might choose the number of books in the classroom, the number of students in the school, the number of tiles on the floor, the number of pages in a particular book, and so forth.

Before students start looking and counting, do at least one example with the class. Count the quantity, then discuss how you would find and label that quantity on the 1000 chart.

There are several different ways students might record each quantity that they find on their 1000 charts. They could write directly on the chart, or run a string or ribbon from the appropriate number on the chart to a description or picture of the thing they found. Some students like to set up a key, as on a map, using color or symbols to link the numbers and the items. For example, they might fill in particular number squares with different colors, explained in a key.

You might establish the following guidelines:

1. Try to find something that matches six different numbers on your 1000 chart.
2. Make sure some of them are lower numbers, some are in the middle, and some are higher numbers.
3. Find at least one thing that is close to 1000.

Some students may want to use numbers they found for the activity in Investigation 2, Multiplying Things in Class, when they searched for grouped things in the classroom (fingers, crayons, chair legs). They may also include things they found at home (in the homework for Session 1).

As students are trying to find their own quantities in the classroom, encourage them to use efficient counting strategies—counting in groups, not by 1's. For example, suggest that they estimate by counting single handfuls or layers, or skip count if something is arranged in an array or equal groups.

If students want to investigate things outside the classroom (such as the number of bricks in the front hall, the number of wheels on cars in the school parking lot, the number of mail slots in the office, the number of students in the school), allow some time for student pairs to go count the particular quantities that interest them.

# Finding Real Quantities for the 1000 Chart

 532 students in the school

 360 boxes of pencils in the storeroom

 960 pages in the dictionary

## Assessment

## Calculating with the 1000 Chart

After students have some confidence about finding quantities on the 1000 chart, have them practice finding "distances" on the chart.

**If I'm at 650, how far do I need to go to get to 1000?**
**How far is it from 325 to 1000? From 320 to 660?**

The purpose of these questions is not to evoke the standard subtraction algorithm, but rather to get students to count by units of 20 or 25 or 100 in going from one point to another, making use of landmarks.

Work on a few of these problems as a whole class, using the larger classroom 1000 chart. Then assign one or two problems to each pair of students. Every student chooses one problem to write up, showing the problem and explaining the solution in a way that would help someone else understand his or her thinking.

You can help students select problems at an appropriate level of difficulty. For example:

Standard problem: How far is it from 350 to 800?

Easier problem: How far is it from 300 to 450?

Harder problem (with "in-between" numbers): How far is it from 480 to 740?

As you observe students' work in class and look over their solutions, you can get a sense of how well each student understands landmarks in the number system up to 1000. Use the following questions to guide your observations:

■ Are students comfortable with reading and writing numbers in the hundreds?

■ Can they skip count across hundreds?

■ Can they use models to help them count (coins, cubes, counting charts)?

■ Can they count comfortably by 25's and 50's, starting with a multiple of that number?

■ Can they use skip counting patterns to help them solve problems?

Read the **Teacher Note**, Assessment: How Far from 650 to 1000? (p. 71) for more ideas on using this assessment.

## Choosing Student Work to Save

As the unit ends, select one of the following options for creating a record of students' work on this unit.

- Students look back through their folders or notebooks and write about what they learned in this unit, what they remember most, what was hard or easy for them. You might have students do this work during their writing time.

- Students select one or two pieces of their work as their best work, and you also choose one or two pieces of their work, to be saved in a portfolio for the year. You might include students' written solutions to the assessment, How Many in 500? (Investigation 2, Session 3), and any other assessment tasks from this unit. Students can create a separate page with brief comments describing each piece of work.

- You may want to send a selection of work home for parents to see. Students write a cover letter, describing their work in this unit. This work should be returned if you are keeping a year-long portfolio of mathematics work for each student.

---

## Assessment: How Far from 650 to 1000?  ◁ Teacher Note

The assessment at the end of this unit (p. 70) checks students' ability to use and understand landmark numbers up to 1000. The following examples of third graders' solutions to this kind of problem show how you might judge their work.

### Latisha's Approach

Latisha easily figures out how far it is from 650 to 1000 by looking at the 1000 chart. She writes:

> I figured out that from 650 to 750 is 100, and if you keep going down to 950, it's 300. There were 50 left then, so I added it to 300 and that made 350.

Latisha seems comfortable with numbers in the hundreds and their relationships to each other. She can count comfortably by 100 from a number that is not a multiple of 100. We might like to ask her more about how she knew that "from 650 to 750 is 100." Did she count? Did she "see" automatically that this distance is 100? Would she be able to figure out the distance from 675 to 775 as easily?

### Michael's Approach

Michael, who also easily finds the distance from 650 to 1000, then works on the more difficult problem, "How far is it from 480 to 740?"

At first he says, "It's 300 and something," as he looks at the hundreds place of both numbers. "Um … maybe 340," he says, now focusing on the numbers in the tens place, "80 and 40 makes 120, so maybe you have to put a 20 with the 300 … 320? 420?"

The teacher recognizes one of Michael's panics about getting the "right answer." Since he easily

*Continued on next page*

solved some of the easier distance problems, the teacher knows he has many of the skills he needs to solve this one. However, his focus on the numerals seems to be interfering with his good numerical reasoning strategies.

The teacher asks Michael to use the 1000 chart to check his answer. He puts one finger on 480 and one on 740.

**Now what are you going to do?**

**Michael:** Count.

**How are you going to count?**

**Michael:** By 1's.

Again, Michael is not calling on the skills he has used in other situations, so the teacher poses another problem.

**It's going to take too long to count by 1's, and it's too easy to make a mistake. What would you do if you wanted to find out how far it is from 60 to 90?**

**Michael** [*promptly*]: 70, 80, 90—that's 30.

**OK, so could you use 10's like that for this one?**

Michael then counts from 480 to 720 by tens, leaving one finger on 480 as he counts. He leaves out one number—"240, 260, 270"—so he ends up with 270. At this point, the teacher has learned enough about Michael's strategies and asks him to write down his solution, both for his portfolio and as a way of getting him to articulate and remember his approach.

Michael is able to operate in the 100's, knows how to count by 10's across multiples of 100, and knows where numbers in the 100's are in relation to each other. However, he is not yet using landmarks (such as 500 and 700, in this case) to help him figure out relationships between numbers. He seems not to be using any visual images to help him "see" the relationships between 480 and 720; rather he focuses on the numerals themselves, which in this case mislead him about the difference between the two numbers.

When using the 1000 chart, Michael still seems intimidated by larger numbers, works very hard to keep track of where he is, and seems worried about losing his place. The teacher decides he needs to work on more of these problems, using the 1000 chart, starting with pairs of numbers that include one multiple of 100. For example, "How far is it from 500 to 720?"

# Counting Around the Class

## Basic Activity

Students count around the class by a particular number. That is, if counting by 2's, the first student says "2," the next student says "4," the next "6," and so forth. Before the count starts, students try to predict on what number the count will end. During and after the count, students discuss relationships between the chosen factor and its multiples.

Counting Around the Class is designed to give students practice with counting by many different numbers and to foster numerical reasoning about the relationships among factors and their multiples. Students focus on:

- becoming familiar with multiplication patterns
- relating factors to their multiples
- developing number sense about multiplication and division relationships

## Materials

- Calculators (for variation)

## Procedure

**Step 1. Choose a number to count by.** For example, if the class has been working with quarters recently, you might want to count by 25's.

**Step 2. Ask students to predict the target number.** "If we count by 25's around the class, what number will we end up on?" Encourage students to talk about how they could figure this out without doing the actual counting.

**Step 3. Count around the class by your chosen number**. "25 … 50 … 75 …" If some students seem uncertain about what comes next, you might put the numbers on the board as they count; seeing the visual patterns can help some students with the spoken one.

You might count around a second time by the same number, starting with a different person, so that students will hear the pattern more than once and have their turns at different points in the sequence.

**Step 4. Pause in the middle of the count to look back.** "We're up to 375 counting by 25's. How many students have we counted so far? How do you know?"

**Step 5. Extend the problem.** Ask questions like these: "Which of your predictions were reasonable? Which were possible? Which were impossible?" (A student might remark, for example, "You couldn't have 510 for 25's because 25 only lands on the 25's, the 50's, the 75's, and the 100's.")

"What if we had 32 students in this class instead of 28? Then where would we end up?"

"What if we used a different number? This time we counted by 25's and ended on 700; what if we counted by 50's? What number do you think we would end on? Why do you think it will be twice as big? How did you figure that out?"

## Variations

**Multiplication Practice**   Use single-digit numbers to provide practice with multiplication (that is, count by 2's, 3's, 4's, 5's, 7's, and so forth). In counting by numbers other than 1, students usually first become comfortable with 2's, 5's, and 10's, which have very regular patterns. Soon they can begin to count by more difficult single-digit numbers: 3, 4, 6, and (later) 7, 8, and 9.

**Landmark Numbers**   When students are learning about money or about our base ten system of numeration, they can count by 20's, 25's, 50's, 100's, and 1000's. Counting by multiples of 10 and 100 (30's, 40's, 600's) will support students' growing familiarity with the base 10 system.

*Continued on next page*

**Making Connections** When you choose harder numbers, pick those that are related in some way to numbers students are very familiar with. For example, once students are comfortable counting by 25's, have them count by 75's. Ask students how knowing the 25's will help them count by 75's. If students are fluent with 3's, try counting by 6's or by 30's. If students are fluent with 10's and 20's, start working on 15's. If they are comfortable counting by 15's, ask them to count by 150's or 1500's.

**Large Numbers** Introduce large numbers, such as 2000, 5000, 1500, or 10,000, so that students begin to work with combinations of these less familiar numbers.

**Using the Calculator** On some days you might have everyone use a calculator, or have a few students use the calculators to skip count while you are counting around the class. On most calculators, the equals (=) key provides a built-in constant function, allowing you to skip count easily. For example, if you want to skip count by 25's, you press your starting number (let's say 0), the operation you want to use (in this case, +), and the number you want to count by (in this case, 25). Then, press the equals key each time you want to add 25. So, if you press

| 0 | + | 25 | = | = | = | = |

you will see on your screen 25, 50, 75, 100.

## Special Notes
**Letting Students Prepare** When introducing an unfamiliar number to count with, students may need some preparation before they try to count around the class. Ask students to work in pairs to figure out, with whatever materials they want to use, what number the count will end on.

**Avoiding Competition** It is important to be sensitive to potential embarrassment or competition if some students have difficulty figuring out their number. One teacher allowed students to volunteer for the next number, rather than counting in a particular order. Other teachers have made the count a cooperative effort, establishing an atmosphere in which students readily helped each other, and anyone felt free to ask for help.

## Related Homework Options
**Counting Patterns** Students write out a counting pattern up to a target number (for example, by 25's up to 500). Then they write about what patterns they see in their counting. Calculators can be used for this.

**Mystery Number Problems** Provide an ending number and ask students to figure out what factor they would have to count by to reach it. For example: "I'm thinking of a mystery number. I figured out that if we counted around the class by my mystery number today, we would get to 2800. What is the mystery number?"

Or, you might provide students with the final number and the factor, and ask them to figure out the number of students in the class. "When a certain class counts by 25's, the last student says 550. How many students are in the class?" Calculators can be used.

# Calendar Math

## Basic Activity

Students try to find numerical expressions that are equal to the day's date. For example, if the date is March 19, students look for ways to combine numbers and operations to make 19. Constraints on what numbers or operations they can use push students in developing their arithmetic skills. Discoveries of principles for "expressions that work" become a part of the class's mathematics culture.

Calendar Math is a simple way of providing arithmetic practice and opportunities for students to share mathematical discoveries. Students focus on:

- developing a web of numerical knowledge about any number
- using operations flexibly
- recognizing relationships among operations (for example, that adding and then subtracting the same number has a net effect of 0)
- learning about and using key mathematical ideas, such as the effect of using an operation with 0 or 1
- deriving new numerical expressions by modifying a particular expression systematically (for example, if 2 + 9 = 11, then so does 3 + 8, 4 + 7, 5 + 6, and so forth)

## Materials

- Calculators (for variation)

## Procedure

**Step 1. Pose the problem.** For example, "Today's date is September 12. Who can think of a way we could combine numbers to make 12?"

**Step 2. List student responses.** Their ideas might include expressions like these:

|  |  |  |
|---|---|---|
| 6 + 6 | 4 × 3 | 12 + 0 |
| ½ × 24 | 3 + (−3) + 6 + 6 | |

**Step 3. Choose a "favorite expression" for the day.** Students choose their favorite from the listed expressions, perhaps the most unusual, or one that uses a new idea. Use the class favorite to write the date on the board: September (0 × 12) + 12.

## Variations

**Introducing Constraints** Introduce constraints based on your class's ease with particular operations and numbers. For example, if students are very comfortable with addition, eliminate addition as a possibility: "Today you can use any operation you want to use, *except* addition." You could also require that a certain operation or kind of number is used. Possible constraints include these:

> You can't use any number that's a multiple of 2.
>
> You can't use addition or subtraction.
>
> You must use more than one operation.
>
> You must use one number that's bigger than 100 (1000, 5000).
>
> You must start with 100.
>
> You must use at least three numbers.
>
> You can't use 0.
>
> You must use at least one number that is smaller than 1.
>
> You must use one negative number.
>
> You can only use 1's, 2's, 3's, and 4's.

**Looking for Patterns** Encourage students to find expressions that they can alter systematically to find more expressions. Here is a pattern that a student came up with for 20:

> 2 × 10, 2 × 9 + 2, 2 × 8 + 4, 2 × 7 + 6 …

**Developing Class "Rules"** Our experience is that, through this activity, new ideas about numbers become part of the culture of the classroom. For example, in one classroom, one student learned about square numbers and the notation for them. Because she used these num-

*Continued on next page*

bers in Calendar Math, other students became familiar with them and were soon using numbers such as $4^2$.

Other kinds of relationships are often discovered by one child and then become common knowledge. For example, one day when a class was finding expressions equivalent to 14, one student suggested "14 times 0." This remark prompted a discussion of what happens when you multiply a number by 0, and students eventually concluded that the result of multiplying any number by zero is 0. The teacher wrote this on a list of "rules" discovered over the course of the year. Following are some other rules students have discovered during this activity:

A number divided by 1 is the number.

A number multiplied by 1 is the number.

Any number multiplied by 0 is 0.

Any number divided by itself is 1.

Subtract or add 0 to any number and you still have the same number.

Adding lots of 0's doesn't change anything.

You can make any number by adding enough 1's to count up to that number.

Adding a number and then subtracting the same number is like adding 0.

**Using the Calculator**  For a quiet ten minutes, have students work individually or in pairs on coming up with ways to make the date, using their calculators. Make sure that they record their work on a piece of paper. They can choose their favorite solution and write it on the board. This is a good way for students to explore new keys on the calculator.

## Related Homework Options

**Planning Ahead**  Suggest that students think at home about how they might make the next day's date. Tell students what constraints they are under, and ask them to figure out five different ways to make the date. They can share their favorite in class.

The following activities will help ensure that this unit is comprehensible to students who are acquiring English as a second language. The suggested approach is based on *The Natural Approach: Language Acquisition in the Classroom* by Stephen D. Krashen and Tracy D. Terrell (Alemany Press, 1983). The intent is for second-language learners to acquire new vocabulary in an active, meaningful context.

Note that *acquiring* a word is different from *learning* a word. Depending on their level of proficiency, students may be able to comprehend a word upon hearing it during an investigation, without being able to say it. Other students may be able to use the word orally, but not read or write it. The goal is to help students naturally acquire targeted vocabulary at their present level of proficiency.

We suggest using these activities just before the related investigations. The activities can also be led by English-proficient students.

### Investigations 1–3

*the numbers 1 to 100*

1. Create action commands that ask students to nonverbally identify numbers written on the board.

   **Put your finger on the number 6.**

   **Cover the number 13.**

2. Use classroom items (paper clips, rubber bands) to help students count to 100.

*divide, equal, unequal, group*

1. Divide 10 pencils in two equal groups. Identify the piles as equal by showing how each group has an *equal* number of pencils.

2. Divide the pencils into two unequal piles. Shake your head as you explain that these groups have an *unequal* number of pencils.

3. Repeat the same procedure, using other classroom items (books, paper clips).

4. Challenge students to demonstrate comprehension of these words by following action commands.

   **Divide these pencils into two equal groups.**

**Divide these paper clips into three equal groups.**

**Divide these books into four unequal groups.**

*money: coins, cents, nickel, dime, quarter, dollar*

1. Use a dollar, quarter, dime, and nickel along with action commands to help familiarize students with these words.

   **Put a quarter in your hand.**

   **Give me a dime.**

   **Put the nickel under the dollar.**

   **Put all the coins in a pile.**

   **Fold the dollar in half.**

2. Create action commands that require students to identify coins by their value.

   **Take a coin that is worth 5 cents.**

   **Give me a coin that is worth 10 cents.**

   **Show me which coin is worth the most money.**

*pattern*

1. Start a clapping pattern (hit knees, hit knees, clap; hit knees, hit knees, clap). Ask students to join in. Then change the pattern.

   **Try this pattern with me.**

   **Who wants to show us a new pattern?**

2. Give students two colors of interlocking cubes. Show them a pattern of cubes in a line, such as blue, red, red, blue, red, red. Ask students to make their own patterns.

3. Draw or write patterns on the board, identify them, and ask students to continue them.

   **This is a pattern of shapes; what comes next?**
   □ △ ○ □ △ ○ □ △ ○

   **This is a pattern in numbers; what comes next?** [*Write the numbers in order, then circle and say aloud each even number, pausing at 8.*]

   1 ②  3 ④  5 ⑥  7 ⑧  9  10  11  12 ...

   **This is another kind of number pattern; what comes next?** [*Write the numbers in a column.*]

   3
   13
   23
   33
   43

# Blackline Masters

Family Letter
*Student Sheet 1*, Ways to Make 20
*Student Sheet 2*, Ways to Make ___
*Student Sheet 3*, Factors of 24
*Student Sheet 4*, Factors of 36
*Student Sheet 5*, Factors of 48
*Student Sheet 6*, Miniature 100 Charts
*Student Sheet 7*, Factors of 100
*Student Sheet 8*, A Picture of 100
*Student Sheet 9*, Ways to Split Up a Dollar
*Student Sheet 10*, Exploring Multiples of 100
*Student Sheet 11*, Calculator Skip Counting
*Student Sheet 12*, Multiplying Things in Class
100 Chart
300 Chart
Money Problems
More Money Problems
Division Problems
One-Centimeter Graph Paper

# Dear Family,

In mathematics, our class is starting a new unit called *Landmarks in the Hundreds*. This unit will help your child learn about important numbers like 100 and 1000, that we use to find our way around the number system.

First your child will be working with 100—an especially important landmark. Then we'll work with multiples of 100, 200, 300, 400, and so on up to 1000. We'll be doing "skip counting"—that's counting by 2's, or 5's, or 10's, or any other number. The children will work in class, and sometimes at home, doing problems like this one:

> If you count by 2's (2, 4, 6, 8, 10, 12, 14 ...) you eventually land on 100. What other numbers can you count by that will land you exactly on 100? What numbers don't work? How many 2's did you count to get to 100?

Children have very interesting ways to figure out these problems. You can help by asking your child to tell you how he or she got an answer. There are many ways of doing these problems—and no single "right" way. What's important for your child to know is how his or her own way works. This is all part of developing good common sense about ~

We _____ ay ask your child to find groups of things around
the _____ about 200, about 300, and so forth. You can
help _____ ut the number of things you both are finding,
for e.

_____ Do you think that would be close to 100?
_____ ceiling?

Finally, _____ inat you yourself need to estimate or deal with large numbers, please involve your child. Whether you're buying food, or deciding how many tiles to buy to patch the floor, your child probably has some good ideas about how to go about it.

Sincerely,

*[handwritten: 30 copies / Student sheet #1 / 50 copies]*

# Ways to Make 20

Take 20 cubes. Put them in equal groups.
How many different ways can you make 20?
Record your results here.

| **Numbers I tried that will make 20** |
| --- |
| Number of cubes in group: _____ <br> Picture of 20: <br><br><br><br> Count: |
| Number of cubes in group: _____ <br> Picture of 20: <br><br><br><br> Count: |
| Number of cubes in group: _____ <br> Picture of 20: <br><br><br><br> Count: |
| **Numbers I tried that didn't work** |
| |

# Ways to Make _____

Choose a number to write in the blank above.
Find equal groupings that make your number.
Record your results in the chart.

**Note:** In class, we use cubes to make groupings. At home you might use beans, popcorn, pennies, paper clips, pebbles, coins, or dots drawn on paper.

| **Numbers I tried that will make ____** |
|---|
| Number of cubes in group: _____<br>Picture of _____:<br><br><br>Count: |
| Number of cubes in group: _____<br>Picture of _____:<br><br><br>Count: |
| Number of cubes in group: _____<br>Picture of _____:<br><br><br>Count: |
| **Numbers I tried that didn't work** |
| |

© Dale Seymour Publications

# Factors of 24

| 1 | 2 | 3 | 4 | 5 | 6 | 7 | 8 | 9 | 10 |
|---|---|---|---|---|---|---|---|---|----|
| 11 | 12 | 13 | 14 | 15 | 16 | 17 | 18 | 19 | 20 |
| 21 | 22 | 23 | 24 | | | | | | |

_____ is a factor of 24.

How many do you need to make 24? _____

_____ × _____ = 24

| 1 | 2 | 3 | 4 | 5 | 6 | 7 | 8 | 9 | 10 |
|---|---|---|---|---|---|---|---|---|----|
| 11 | 12 | 13 | 14 | 15 | 16 | 17 | 18 | 19 | 20 |
| 21 | 22 | 23 | 24 | | | | | | |

_____ is a factor of 24.

How many do you need to make 24? _____

_____ × _____ = 24

| 1 | 2 | 3 | 4 | 5 | 6 | 7 | 8 | 9 | 10 |
|---|---|---|---|---|---|---|---|---|----|
| 11 | 12 | 13 | 14 | 15 | 16 | 17 | 18 | 19 | 20 |
| 21 | 22 | 23 | 24 | | | | | | |

_____ is a factor of 24.

How many do you need to make 24? _____

_____ × _____ = 24

| 1 | 2 | 3 | 4 | 5 | 6 | 7 | 8 | 9 | 10 |
|---|---|---|---|---|---|---|---|---|----|
| 11 | 12 | 13 | 14 | 15 | 16 | 17 | 18 | 19 | 20 |
| 21 | 22 | 23 | 24 | | | | | | |

_____ is a factor of 24.

How many do you need to make 24? _____

_____ × _____ = 24

# Factors of 36

| 1 | 2 | 3 | 4 | 5 | 6 | 7 | 8 | 9 | 10 |
|---|---|---|---|---|---|---|---|---|----|
| 11 | 12 | 13 | 14 | 15 | 16 | 17 | 18 | 19 | 20 |
| 21 | 22 | 23 | 24 | 25 | 26 | 27 | 28 | 29 | 30 |
| 31 | 32 | 33 | 34 | 35 | 36 | | | | |

\_\_\_\_\_ is a factor of 36.

How many do you need to make 36? \_\_\_\_\_

\_\_\_\_\_ × \_\_\_\_\_ = 36

| 1 | 2 | 3 | 4 | 5 | 6 | 7 | 8 | 9 | 10 |
|---|---|---|---|---|---|---|---|---|----|
| 11 | 12 | 13 | 14 | 15 | 16 | 17 | 18 | 19 | 20 |
| 21 | 22 | 23 | 24 | 25 | 26 | 27 | 28 | 29 | 30 |
| 31 | 32 | 33 | 34 | 35 | 36 | | | | |

\_\_\_\_\_ is a factor of 36.

How many do you need to make 36? \_\_\_\_\_

\_\_\_\_\_ × \_\_\_\_\_ = 36

| 1 | 2 | 3 | 4 | 5 | 6 | 7 | 8 | 9 | 10 |
|---|---|---|---|---|---|---|---|---|----|
| 11 | 12 | 13 | 14 | 15 | 16 | 17 | 18 | 19 | 20 |
| 21 | 22 | 23 | 24 | 25 | 26 | 27 | 28 | 29 | 30 |
| 31 | 32 | 33 | 34 | 35 | 36 | | | | |

\_\_\_\_\_ is a factor of 36.

How many do you need to make 36? \_\_\_\_\_

\_\_\_\_\_ × \_\_\_\_\_ = 36

# Factors of 48

| 1 | 2 | 3 | 4 | 5 | 6 | 7 | 8 | 9 | 10 |
|---|---|---|---|---|---|---|---|---|----|
| 11 | 12 | 13 | 14 | 15 | 16 | 17 | 18 | 19 | 20 |
| 21 | 22 | 23 | 24 | 25 | 26 | 27 | 28 | 29 | 30 |
| 31 | 32 | 33 | 34 | 35 | 36 | 37 | 38 | 39 | 40 |
| 41 | 42 | 43 | 44 | 45 | 46 | 47 | 48 | | |

_____ is a factor of 48.

How many do you need to make 48? _____

_____ × _____ = 48

| 1 | 2 | 3 | 4 | 5 | 6 | 7 | 8 | 9 | 10 |
|---|---|---|---|---|---|---|---|---|----|
| 11 | 12 | 13 | 14 | 15 | 16 | 17 | 18 | 19 | 20 |
| 21 | 22 | 23 | 24 | 25 | 26 | 27 | 28 | 29 | 30 |
| 31 | 32 | 33 | 34 | 35 | 36 | 37 | 38 | 39 | 40 |
| 41 | 42 | 43 | 44 | 45 | 46 | 47 | 48 | | |

_____ is a factor of 48.

How many do you need to make 48? _____

_____ × _____ = 48

| 1 | 2 | 3 | 4 | 5 | 6 | 7 | 8 | 9 | 10 |
|---|---|---|---|---|---|---|---|---|----|
| 11 | 12 | 13 | 14 | 15 | 16 | 17 | 18 | 19 | 20 |
| 21 | 22 | 23 | 24 | 25 | 26 | 27 | 28 | 29 | 30 |
| 31 | 32 | 33 | 34 | 35 | 36 | 37 | 38 | 39 | 40 |
| 41 | 42 | 43 | 44 | 45 | 46 | 47 | 48 | | |

_____ is a factor of 48.

How many do you need to make 48? _____

_____ × _____ = 48

# Miniature 100 Charts

| 1 | 2 | 3 | 4 | 5 | 6 | 7 | 8 | 9 | 10 |
|---|---|---|---|---|---|---|---|---|---|
| 11 | 12 | 13 | 14 | 15 | 16 | 17 | 18 | 19 | 20 |
| 21 | 22 | 23 | 24 | 25 | 26 | 27 | 28 | 29 | 30 |
| 31 | 32 | 33 | 34 | 35 | 36 | 37 | 38 | 39 | 40 |
| 41 | 42 | 43 | 44 | 45 | 46 | 47 | 48 | 49 | 50 |
| 51 | 52 | 53 | 54 | 55 | 56 | 57 | 58 | 59 | 60 |
| 61 | 62 | 63 | 64 | 65 | 66 | 67 | 68 | 69 | 70 |
| 71 | 72 | 73 | 74 | 75 | 76 | 77 | 78 | 79 | 80 |
| 81 | 82 | 83 | 84 | 85 | 86 | 87 | 88 | 89 | 90 |
| 91 | 92 | 93 | 94 | 95 | 96 | 97 | 98 | 99 | 100 |

I counted by _____.

I made _____ jumps to reach 100.

| 1 | 2 | 3 | 4 | 5 | 6 | 7 | 8 | 9 | 10 |
|---|---|---|---|---|---|---|---|---|---|
| 11 | 12 | 13 | 14 | 15 | 16 | 17 | 18 | 19 | 20 |
| 21 | 22 | 23 | 24 | 25 | 26 | 27 | 28 | 29 | 30 |
| 31 | 32 | 33 | 34 | 35 | 36 | 37 | 38 | 39 | 40 |
| 41 | 42 | 43 | 44 | 45 | 46 | 47 | 48 | 49 | 50 |
| 51 | 52 | 53 | 54 | 55 | 56 | 57 | 58 | 59 | 60 |
| 61 | 62 | 63 | 64 | 65 | 66 | 67 | 68 | 69 | 70 |
| 71 | 72 | 73 | 74 | 75 | 76 | 77 | 78 | 79 | 80 |
| 81 | 82 | 83 | 84 | 85 | 86 | 87 | 88 | 89 | 90 |
| 91 | 92 | 93 | 94 | 95 | 96 | 97 | 98 | 99 | 100 |

I counted by _____.

I made _____ jumps to reach 100.

| 1 | 2 | 3 | 4 | 5 | 6 | 7 | 8 | 9 | 10 |
|---|---|---|---|---|---|---|---|---|---|
| 11 | 12 | 13 | 14 | 15 | 16 | 17 | 18 | 19 | 20 |
| 21 | 22 | 23 | 24 | 25 | 26 | 27 | 28 | 29 | 30 |
| 31 | 32 | 33 | 34 | 35 | 36 | 37 | 38 | 39 | 40 |
| 41 | 42 | 43 | 44 | 45 | 46 | 47 | 48 | 49 | 50 |
| 51 | 52 | 53 | 54 | 55 | 56 | 57 | 58 | 59 | 60 |
| 61 | 62 | 63 | 64 | 65 | 66 | 67 | 68 | 69 | 70 |
| 71 | 72 | 73 | 74 | 75 | 76 | 77 | 78 | 79 | 80 |
| 81 | 82 | 83 | 84 | 85 | 86 | 87 | 88 | 89 | 90 |
| 91 | 92 | 93 | 94 | 95 | 96 | 97 | 98 | 99 | 100 |

I counted by _____.

I made _____ jumps to reach 100.

# Factors of 100

Use this recording sheet with the Miniature 100 Charts.

| Numbers we tried | Did you land on 100 exactly? | | If it worked: How many in 100? |
|---|---|---|---|
| _____ | Yes | No | _____ |
| _____ | Yes | No | _____ |
| _____ | Yes | No | _____ |
| _____ | Yes | No | _____ |
| _____ | Yes | No | _____ |
| _____ | Yes | No | _____ |
| _____ | Yes | No | _____ |
| _____ | Yes | No | _____ |
| _____ | Yes | No | _____ |
| _____ | Yes | No | _____ |
| _____ | Yes | No | _____ |
| _____ | Yes | No | _____ |
| _____ | Yes | No | _____ |
| _____ | Yes | No | _____ |
| _____ | Yes | No | _____ |
| _____ | Yes | No | _____ |
| _____ | Yes | No | _____ |
| _____ | Yes | No | _____ |
| _____ | Yes | No | _____ |

# A Picture of 100

HOMEWORK

Make a picture of 100 of the same thing.

You might draw 100 things.
Or, you might glue 100 of something small
onto a sheet of paper.

Arrange the 100 things in equal groups.
Make it easy to see that you have 100 things
on your paper.

Remember the picture of 100 you made in class?
Use groups of a **different** size.

Your family can help you make this picture.

# Ways to Split Up a Dollar

| Number of People Sharing a Dollar | How Much Each Person Gets |
|---|---|
|  |  |
|  |  |
|  |  |
|  |  |
|  |  |
|  |  |
|  |  |
|  |  |
|  |  |
|  |  |
|  |  |
|  |  |
| Cannot split a dollar evenly: | |

# Exploring Multiples of 100

Choose one of these factors of 100. Circle it.

4    5    10    20    25

Then fill in the chart.

Show how many of your number makes 100, 200, and 300.

You can go further if you want to.

| | How many? |
|---|---|
| 100 | _____ |
| 200 | _____ |
| 300 | _____ |
| _____ | _____ |
| _____ | _____ |
| _____ | _____ |
| _____ | _____ |
| _____ | _____ |
| _____ | _____ |

I know there are _____ in 300 because _____

_____

_____

_____

_____

This is what we notice about the patterns in our list:

_____

_____

_____

_____

# Calculator Skip Counting

Choose a number to count by. Pick one you think will land exactly on 300.

Skip count by this number on your calculator.

Does it work? If so, write how many of your number it takes to get to 300.

| Numbers we tried | Did you land on 300 exactly? | If it worked: How many in 300? |
|---|---|---|
| _____ | Yes   No | _____ |
| _____ | Yes   No | _____ |
| _____ | Yes   No | _____ |
| _____ | Yes   No | _____ |
| _____ | Yes   No | _____ |
| _____ | Yes   No | _____ |
| _____ | Yes   No | _____ |
| _____ | Yes   No | _____ |
| _____ | Yes   No | _____ |
| _____ | Yes   No | _____ |
| _____ | Yes   No | _____ |
| _____ | Yes   No | _____ |
| _____ | Yes   No | _____ |
| _____ | Yes   No | _____ |
| _____ | Yes   No | _____ |
| _____ | Yes   No | _____ |
| _____ | Yes   No | _____ |
| _____ | Yes   No | _____ |

# Multiplying Things in Class

Find something in the classroom that comes in groups.
Each group should have the same amount.
Figure out how many there are altogether in the classroom.

Try to find things that total in the hundreds.
Are there nearly 200? nearly 300? nearly 400?

For example, how many fingers are there in the room?
Count by 10's to find the total.

Here are some other things you might look for:

- boxes of paper clips
- packages or pads of paper
- packs of pencils
- chair and desk legs
- rows of bricks or tiles

# 100 Chart

| 1 | 2 | 3 | 4 | 5 | 6 | 7 | 8 | 9 | 10 |
|---|---|---|---|---|---|---|---|---|---|
| 11 | 12 | 13 | 14 | 15 | 16 | 17 | 18 | 19 | 20 |
| 21 | 22 | 23 | 24 | 25 | 26 | 27 | 28 | 29 | 30 |
| 31 | 32 | 33 | 34 | 35 | 36 | 37 | 38 | 39 | 40 |
| 41 | 42 | 43 | 44 | 45 | 46 | 47 | 48 | 49 | 50 |
| 51 | 52 | 53 | 54 | 55 | 56 | 57 | 58 | 59 | 60 |
| 61 | 62 | 63 | 64 | 65 | 66 | 67 | 68 | 69 | 70 |
| 71 | 72 | 73 | 74 | 75 | 76 | 77 | 78 | 79 | 80 |
| 81 | 82 | 83 | 84 | 85 | 86 | 87 | 88 | 89 | 90 |
| 91 | 92 | 93 | 94 | 95 | 96 | 97 | 98 | 99 | 100 |

## 300 Chart

| 1 | 2 | 3 | 4 | 5 | 6 | 7 | 8 | 9 | 10 |
|---|---|---|---|---|---|---|---|---|---|
| 11 | 12 | 13 | 14 | 15 | 16 | 17 | 18 | 19 | 20 |
| 21 | 22 | 23 | 24 | 25 | 26 | 27 | 28 | 29 | 30 |
| 31 | 32 | 33 | 34 | 35 | 36 | 37 | 38 | 39 | 40 |
| 41 | 42 | 43 | 44 | 45 | 46 | 47 | 48 | 49 | 50 |
| 51 | 52 | 53 | 54 | 55 | 56 | 57 | 58 | 59 | 60 |
| 61 | 62 | 63 | 64 | 65 | 66 | 67 | 68 | 69 | 70 |
| 71 | 72 | 73 | 74 | 75 | 76 | 77 | 78 | 79 | 80 |
| 81 | 82 | 83 | 84 | 85 | 86 | 87 | 88 | 89 | 90 |
| 91 | 92 | 93 | 94 | 95 | 96 | 97 | 98 | 99 | 100 |
| 101 | 102 | 103 | 104 | 105 | 106 | 107 | 108 | 109 | 110 |
| 111 | 112 | 113 | 114 | 115 | 116 | 117 | 118 | 119 | 120 |
| 121 | 122 | 123 | 124 | 125 | 126 | 127 | 128 | 129 | 130 |
| 131 | 132 | 133 | 134 | 135 | 136 | 137 | 138 | 139 | 140 |
| 141 | 142 | 143 | 144 | 145 | 146 | 147 | 148 | 149 | 150 |
| 151 | 152 | 153 | 154 | 155 | 156 | 157 | 158 | 159 | 160 |
| 161 | 162 | 163 | 164 | 165 | 166 | 167 | 168 | 169 | 170 |
| 171 | 172 | 173 | 174 | 175 | 176 | 177 | 178 | 179 | 180 |
| 181 | 182 | 183 | 184 | 185 | 186 | 187 | 188 | 189 | 190 |
| 191 | 192 | 193 | 194 | 195 | 196 | 197 | 198 | 199 | 200 |
| 201 | 202 | 203 | 204 | 205 | 206 | 207 | 208 | 209 | 210 |
| 211 | 212 | 213 | 214 | 215 | 216 | 217 | 218 | 219 | 220 |
| 221 | 222 | 223 | 224 | 225 | 226 | 227 | 228 | 229 | 230 |
| 231 | 232 | 233 | 234 | 235 | 236 | 237 | 238 | 239 | 240 |
| 241 | 242 | 243 | 244 | 245 | 246 | 247 | 248 | 249 | 250 |
| 251 | 252 | 253 | 254 | 255 | 256 | 257 | 258 | 259 | 260 |
| 261 | 262 | 263 | 264 | 265 | 266 | 267 | 268 | 269 | 270 |
| 271 | 272 | 273 | 274 | 275 | 276 | 277 | 278 | 279 | 280 |
| 281 | 282 | 283 | 284 | 285 | 286 | 287 | 288 | 289 | 290 |
| 291 | 292 | 293 | 294 | 295 | 296 | 297 | 298 | 299 | 300 |

| How many quarters are there in $3.75? | How many quarters are there in $4.25? |
| How much money do I have if I have 17 quarters? | How much money is 23 quarters? |
| How many dimes are there in $4.30? | How much money is 13 quarters? |
| How much money is 27 dimes? | How many nickels are there in $3.75? |

You have $3.75. Pencils cost a quarter each.

How many pencils can you buy?

Ten people got on the bus. Each paid 75 cents.

How much did the bus driver collect from them?

The early show at the movies costs $2.50.

How much will four friends pay to go to the early show?

Someone had $6.00 in two pockets. There was $3.75 in one pocket.

How much was in the other pocket?

Suppose each person in class today had a quarter in his or her pocket.

How much money would we have?

I want to bring my friends with me to the swimming pool. The pool charges 75 cents for each person. I saved up $9.75.

How many friends can I invite?

# Division Problems

There are 380 students in a school. There are about 20 students in each class.

How many classes are there?

I counted the wheels in the school parking lot. There were 84 wheels.

How many cars were in the parking lot?

I'm baking cookies. I want to make about 250 cookies. I can bake 25 cookies in a batch.

How many batches should I make?

Some students had a cookie sale. They sold chocolate chip cookies for 5 cents each. They earned $4.60.

How many cookies did they sell?

There are 390 students in a school. There are about 30 students in each class.

How many classes are there?

Two friends had a lemonade stand. They charged 15 cents for each glass. One day, they sold enough to get $1.80.

How many glasses did they sell?